THE DNA OF A DOCTOR

THE DNA OF A DOCTOR

HOW UPBRINGING, CULTURE, AND UNBRIDLED AMBITION CURATES ACHIEVEMENT

SMITA R. RAMANADHAM, MD
BOARD-CERTIFIED PLASTIC & RECONSTRUCTIVE SURGEON

A POST HILL PRESS BOOK
ISBN: 979-8-89565-215-2
ISBN (eBook): 979-8-89565-216-9

The DNA of a Doctor:
How Upbringing, Culture, and Unbridled Ambition Curates Achievement

Cover design by Conroy Accord

Post Hill Press
New York • Nashville
posthillpress.com

Published in the United States of America
1 2 3 4 5 6 7 8 9 10

To my dad, my hero, who taught me to always dream big, always trust in God, and always do the hard work.

To my mom, who broke barriers without realizing it, whose love for medicine and compassion for her patients continues to inspire me to this day.

To my husband for always being my biggest supporter and advocate.

To my brother who has been by my side since day one.

To my mentors, thank you for pushing me to be better than I thought I could ever be.

And to all the young aspiring doctors. Walk through every door that has been opened for you, and always push to walk though more, but, most important, always extend a hand to those that follow.

Contents

Introduction

Be who you were created to be, and
you will set the world on fire.
—St. Catherine of Siena

As a plastic surgeon, people ask me all the time: What's your favorite surgery? The truth is that I don't have one. I like them all—because ideally every surgery I do leads to one ultimate result for my patients: *confidence*. When I meet a prospective patient for the first time for consultation, so many women are nervous and insecure about their area of concern. Some live their lives wearing heavy makeup to hide their facial "flaws" from the world—including from me, the surgeon. Others hide their bodies under baggy clothes. Even as I'm doing the physical exam on the area in question, they are trying to hide that certain part of their body.

And then, when they come back for their follow-up appointment post-surgery, they are a brand-new person. They walk into the room, heads held high. They have a smile on their refreshed faces. They're excited to show off the results and their new bodies. Frequently they will sit on the table happily chatting half-naked, to the point where either the nurse or I will say, "OK, you can get dressed now." The difference is like night and day.

This transformation, in a nutshell, is why I do what I do: I can help my patients to boost or regain their confidence. Because I can help them to look their best, they can go on to give their best. At work, at home, in their dating lives or marriage, and every social interaction. By using my medical and surgical skills to give patients a new lease on life, I am helping to make women and men not only look good but feel good, strong, and empowered. Both inside and out. That is always my ultimate goal and why I love performing plastic surgery.

***

I am a statistical rarity in my specialty, as plastic surgery is an extremely male-dominated field. The latest statistics show that only 17 percent of board-certified plastic surgeons in the country are female, while 92 percent of our patients are, which is quite a disconnect. Where I have established my own practice, with two offices in New Jersey, there are only a handful of female board-certified plastic surgeons in the entire state.

I find there are certain advantages to being in this female minority—there is absolutely a level of comfort for women to have a doctor who truly understands what their body has been through. When they talk about wanting their old breasts back, the struggles of weight fluctuations and the consequences on their bodies, hormonal changes, or the sagging and lines around their eyes, they know they're talking to someone who truly understands those issues on a core level—and oftentimes experiences these same concerns herself.

Not only am I a woman, I am also Indian. My friend and fellow plastic surgeon Ashley and I created a podcast: as female plastic surgeons are such a rarity, we thought it was important to have visibility and represent our field. We started on Instagram Live and, what surprised me after our first appearance, and every other time subsequently, was the number of direct messages (DMs) I received from Indian medical and pre-med students all over the country. I even heard from young aspiring doctors in India saying, "I've never seen an Indian female plastic surgeon…I never thought anybody like me could become one." If you don't see it, it's hard to imagine that you could be it. Whatever that "it" is for you. For me, I'm so happy to be able to inspire others to chase their dreams of becoming a surgeon, plastic or otherwise.

Not that South Asians are a rarity in medicine; quite the opposite. Next to Caucasians, Asian Americans are the second-highest demographic in medicine; accounting for 17 percent of doctors in 2018. However, in the surgical subspecialty, particularly plastic surgery, we are very much a tiny minority. We are such a small number that it's hard to find reliable figures on how many female Indian plastic surgeons are currently practicing.

Certainly, that ratio is improving every year, which is gratifying for me, as I know from experience the pressures these young women are facing. Indian culture places a great deal of value on education, and medicine is a highly regarded and well-respected field. But the large percentage of Indian doctors does not translate to plastic surgery, particularly for women. That is because there is an even stronger focus in our culture on having a family. A spouse and children are just as valuable as a career in medicine.

So, how does a young woman balance being a doctor and having a family? Many choose to become MDs but forego the time-consuming decade and punishing schedule of pursuing a surgical specialty during their most fertile years. Many choose internal medicine or pediatrics, for example, demanding fields in their own right, but with more flexibility in terms of setting regular hours. These tracks of medicine are equally rewarding yet allow a better work–life balance as the hours are more aligned with what we consider the "norm." But I chose a different path. We all have our path to follow, and while family and marriage were important to me, I felt a deeper calling for my life's purpose. At least, it was one I needed to pursue before focusing on a family.

***

I was a quiet child: timid and studious and a real daddy's girl. As a kid at social gatherings, I would literally hang on to my dad's pants leg most of the day and refuse to join the other, rowdier kids playing across the room. I was much too shy to even approach them. I became more outgoing in college, like many young adults do, but my turning point certainly came during my surgical residency, which is a brutal training ground that will toughen anybody up. My program was comparable to a military bootcamp, designed to weed out the weak. During this time, you're in pure survival mode, running on no sleep and constant stress. You are trying to save patients who are literally dying on you. As you progress through the years you simply must rise to the occasion, become more assertive and start delegating and handing out orders. Lives depend on it.

As for surgeons, in the operating room (OR) there's an anesthesiologist present, but the surgeon is the head of the team. If anything goes wrong, everyone looks to me. Surgeons have to be the leader in the room, and while plenty of students going into their surgical residency have leadership in their personality, mine was not innate. Projecting confidence and leadership was a skill I had to develop throughout medical school in order to make it into a good program. The need for this trait was only reinforced during my residencies. Perhaps the ability was always in me, but my training forced this aspect of my personality to emerge. It's the only way to succeed on this path.

And then, after years and years of single-mindedly pursuing my goals, I was an experienced plastic surgeon with an excellent position at a major research hospital in a big city when I came to a gradual realization: I just wasn't fulfilled. There were several reasons, but mostly it boiled down to feeling—stifled. Believe me when I tell you that surgeons are careful planners, with backup plans for backup plans for every conceivable contingency, but I was in my mid-thirties, dating, and had no alternative plan for the rest of my career, due to the fact that all my schooling and training was in medicine. I was at such a low that I truly questioned if I had made the wrong choice altogether in choosing plastic surgery as my profession, but there was no other career I felt remotely qualified to explore. The one option I had never even considered was going out on my own and starting a solo practice. Yet that's what I eventually did. After *four years* of debate and careful deliberation!

There were plenty of naysayers along the way. Friends and relatives had strong opinions they were happy to share with me. This was not entirely new, of course. I'd had lots of input on choices my entire life, much good, some bad. I'd come a long way with developing my inner will and growing confidence, but this would be an entirely new journey with plenty of unexpected bumps and hard lessons along the way. At the end of the day, for me, everything has to do with confidence. The confidence to know when to say yes and, more important, when to say no.

The confidence to upend expectations and forge your own path. The confidence to take your seat at the table—whatever table that may be.

My journey led me to my absolute dream job, which is far more than a job to me. It's a calling. As a plastic surgeon with my own practice, I am doing what I was meant to do. Instilling that feeling of confidence in others. That confidence gives my patients a new lease on life; it is without a doubt my life's purpose.

Chapter One

It All Started with an American Dream

I am sure that all first-generation Indians have heard their parents tell a story something like this. Here's mine: my father came to America with seven dollars in his pocket. Literally seven dollars! On that twenty-hour flight in 1975, Dad splurged and bought a pack of cigarettes on the airplane. This meant that when he landed, he was down to six precious dollars to start his brand-new life.

Many Indian immigrants were making their way to the United States in the mid-seventies, and most landed in the New York area and settled nearby. The community was small, but Indians have always had the uncanny ability to find each other and make America feel like the home they left behind. Dad happened to land in Newark, New Jersey, and found a job at a small local pharmacy, where he worked as a pharmacy tech. He rented a room from an older Portuguese couple, who provided not only a roof over his head but hot meals, too, in the culturally diverse Iron Bound district of Newark. He worked all the hours he possibly could, studied for his American pharmacy exams and saved up his money.

After a few years he was finally in the position to start thinking about settling down. He had taken and passed his US pharmacy licensing exams and become acclimated to life in the States. He was also now able to afford to move out on his own. So, Dad returned to India to see his family and meet the women they wanted to set him up with. He headed back to Mangalagiri, the tiny village where he'd grown up, in the Guntur district of Andhra Pradesh.

Dad was one of three brothers, the middle child, and was always seen as the runt of the family. He had asthma as a child and was always the sickly one. Living in a hot, dusty, small village without any real medical care or treatments only made his exacerbations more frequent.

Though Mangalagiri was small, my grandfather was well-established there. He was a big fish in a small pond and on the board of trustees for the area's one school, which housed the equivalent of kindergarten to high school. He also owned several movie theaters and was not only well known in his town but in surrounding areas, as well. In my grandfather's mind, Dad was always going to be the son who would grow up and take over the family businesses. Because of that, my grandfather felt there was absolutely no need for my father to pursue a higher education.

Dad had his own dreams, however. He wanted to get an education, become a surgeon, and move to America, where he would create an amazing new life for his future kids. He knew he would have to do this without the support of his parents, so Dad started preparations to escape his destiny early. He took a secret side job and started saving money in high school; his parents had no idea. He needed to be able to pay his college and schooling fees on his own.

In India at that time, the next educational level after high school was earning a BSc, a three-year bachelor of science, similar to an American four-year college degree. Once he graduated high school and had saved just enough money, my dad ran away from home and headed to northern India. He had no real game plan other than determination and a will to enroll in a bachelor of science program. But he didn't make it far from the train station initially as he was conserving money and trying to come up with his next step. He ate one small meal a day, washing up in the public bathroom and sleeping on the benches at night.

Dad's native language was Telugu, but in northern India the predominant language was Hindi. While most educated people spoke Hindi (the national language) and English, hearing your own tongue was always familiar and comforting. One day, he happened to overhear a couple speaking Telugu, so he made a beeline toward the familiar sound. The couple was happy to meet him and asked what he was doing so far from home. When Dad explained his situation, the woman mentioned there was a college nearby. "Go to this school and ask to speak to the headmaster's wife. She is Telugu, and she will help you," the woman advised.

Dad cleaned up and got himself over to this school, where he managed to talk his way into meeting the headmaster's wife, who did indeed help him enroll. He studied there for the next several years and earned his degree; along the way his family eventually reconciled themselves to his insistence on higher education. As he was finishing his BSc, Dad, along with every other graduating student, had to take a qualifying exam to further his education. Based on the results of this one test, each student would earn a place to study medicine, or science, or whatever field he hoped to pursue. He took the all-important exam and returned home to his village for holiday break.

The form letter sent to all students announcing exam results was short and straightforward. "You earned a seat in X" (whatever the desired specialty might be) with a deadline to report, enroll, and pay the fees. Upon his return after the holiday break, he found the letter in his room saying that he had earned a seat in medicine. But it was too late. He had missed the deadline, and his place had been given to someone else. However, there happened to still be an opening available in pharmacy, which he took, gladly. Still, a part of his dream died that day, knowing he would never become a surgeon. Dad entered pharmacy school, earned his advanced degree, and created a new goal and dream for himself. Perhaps bigger than his original.

Reflection:

I was always too young, too distracted and too focused on my own career goals to really understand the magnitude of what my dad had done at such a young age. He was in his late teens when he ran away from home to educate himself. Today, kids run away from home for the wrong reasons more often than the right ones. Dad just wanted an education. This desire had certainly not been ingrained in him as it was in me (by him and Mom). Maybe it was watching movies in his own father's theaters that made him realize that life and the world was much bigger than what his small village could offer.

Dad always wanted more in life and was determined to make it happen. He sacrificed everything, left his family, left all that was familiar behind. He could have lost everything and failed. He was rerouted along the way a few times, but through blood, sweat, and tears he made his dream happen. He didn't have a choice. He and my mom created a better world for their children—my brother and me. I could never have done what he did, but I learned from him. He planted a seed that I would use so many years later. To dream big.

Dad's journey was just one story in a much larger cultural shift. The mid-1970s marked a crucial period for Indian immigration to the United States, fueled by the 1965 Immigration and Nationality Act, which opened the United States to many countries previously restricted, including India. This wave brought a significant number of skilled professionals who, along with their families, formed new communities and established businesses while navigating the challenges of cultural adaptation and social integration.

Meanwhile, in another small village several hours away—Gudlavalleru in the Krishna district of Andhra Pradesh—my mom was born to a mother who carried children sixteen times. My grandmother had married at the age of eleven or twelve; the groom, my grandfather, was not that much older. That was the culture in that time and place; once girls had their period, they left and started their own families. My grandparents were kids having their own kids. Eight of their sixteen children did not survive—either miscarried, stillborn, or died in infancy. There was very little healthcare in their small village; certainly, no prenatal care, pediatric specialists, or anything remotely similar.

Due to the lost pregnancies, the surviving eight children were spread far apart in age, with my mom the second oldest of a group of five who were separated by many years from the other four older siblings. At the time Mom was growing up, her older brothers and sisters had already married, moved out, and were living in their own households. But, for the four youngest children—my mother and her three younger brothers—my grandmother had a different plan.

My grandfather was a farmer and my grandmother a traditional homemaker. However, she was a bright and capable woman; she became an unofficial "banker" in their tiny village by making micro loans. She started with a few rupees, enough to advance small sums to a few friends and neighbors, hoping just to earn a bit of money from the interest to help with household expenses. My grandmother had a "side hustle" before that was even a thing! Eventually she made quite a success of this home business based on community relationships and became a somewhat prominent figure in the village.

With that venture going well, and now much older and wiser than the teenager who'd started bearing children so early, my grandmother realized it was time to make a change. For her youngest kids—those who still lived at home—she had a radical new idea: an education and an entirely different life plan. Her dream was for her younger children to become doctors. So, naturally, an education was of utmost importance.

As a result, my mom spent much of her childhood going to school and studying; that was her life. She would be awakened at three or four in the morning, her mother would prepare food for her and her younger brothers, they would eat, study, and then go to school. They would come home and study some more. While my mom loved sports, that was not a priority. Her mission was to study. The next day, same schedule on repeat. This went on for years and years. And her diligent preparation paid off as her mother wished.

My mother graduated from high school, went off to college and entered medical school at Gandhi Medical College in Hyderabad, a remarkable feat for a young woman from a rural village in India in the 1970s. In the twenty-five years since 1950, sociocultural factors and more training opportunities had led to an increase in the number of female doctors, which had been until then very low compared to men—though rising only to a male-to-female ratio of approximately ten-to-two by the late seventies. There were no female doctors around for my mother to emulate. It was just her calling and my grandmother's dream that fueled her ambition.

When my mom was in her third year of medical school, her mother became ill, and she was summoned home to see her. Mom took a several-month leave of absence from school to be with her mother, my grandmother. Once she passed, my mom made a resolution to stay and help to raise the three youngest boys—and to honor her mother's wishes of them all becoming doctors. Two of these brothers did become doctors. The other went to grad school and took a position with the Indian government. Three out of four—not bad!

Then it was back to finishing her own dream of medicine. After graduating from medical school, Mom was living at home, preparing for her clinicals and figuring out her next step. At this point family members started really putting on the pressure. She was in her mid-twenties and not married. This was considered old for the time and place. Her brothers and uncles were actively seeking matrimonial matches for her. None of these potential suitors interested her, for a number of reasons; mostly because she had her own dreams to chase first.

Reflection:

Role models matter. A European study in 2022 commissioned by LinkedIn revealed that 43 percent of women believe that they would be more successful if they had a role model in the workplace. However, 55 percent of respondents felt there was a lack of relatable role models in their workplace. This is particularly critical in male-dominated fields such as STEM or surgery. Fortunately, I had excellent role models in my own family.

I come from a long line of strong women. There's a saying—"I'm a strong woman because a strong woman raised me"—and that strong woman was raised by another strong woman, my grandmother. I never met my grandmother (Ammamma, as I would have called her); she passed away before my mom was even married but I often wonder if she knew how far her wishes for her own daughter would extend. She created generations of doctors in a family that, until she intervened, had never been educated. Not only did I become a doctor, but my uncle and his two kids are now doctors, too. My brother and other cousins are pharmacists and engineers. My guess is she would not be surprised—if there's one thing I learned from my own mom, it's that my Ammamma had dreams that were far bigger than her own.

***

When Dad returned to India in 1978, he was ready to get married. His family, too, had helpfully been seeking suitable prospects for him. So, while he was home, he held many meetings with potential matches. None of the young women caught his fancy, though. Despite his family's best efforts, no match was made. He had his return flight to America booked and accepted that he would be returning to his new life without a bride.

While waiting at the bus station in Vijayawada, the biggest town near his home village, he struck up a conversation with a young man who was also waiting for the bus to Gudlavalleru. "I'm here from America and I'm looking for matches. I haven't found anybody yet so I'm going back to New York in a couple of days," my dad lamented.

This man happened to be my mom's younger brother, a medical student himself. His interest was sparked by this progressive Indian man forging his own path in a new country. "We're looking for a match for my older sister. She's a doctor," my uncle shared. "Why don't you come home and meet her?"

Dad had nothing to lose. He was stuck waiting for his bus and they just announced a bus strike anyway, so he accompanied this man to the family home and waited patiently to meet my mother. My mother had a medical degree, her own ideas and spoke her mind. But on this occasion, her brothers and uncles made things very clear. She was not to speak; she should not make eye contact with my father (no respectable woman of the time made eye contact with strange men); and there would be no mention of her faith. She simply went along with their wishes—not because she wanted to, but because she had been warned that anything she said could disgrace the family name.

At that time in India during the matchmaking process women were supposed to be meek and silent. The men of the families did all the talking and negotiating. It was a marriage between families, not individuals as it is in the Western world. My dad and my mom's brothers discussed a possible shared future. At a certain point my father asked, "Can I speak with her?" He wanted to get to know her and find out what her wishes were. The brothers all said "No," immediately. Even so, he liked her and agreed to a marriage. Her brothers and uncles approved, and just like that, my parents were married. Four days later. At 4:50 a.m. on April 5, 1978.

***

Both my parents had grown up in Hindu families. Our last name, Ramanadham, is a common traditional Hindu surname. Both my grandmothers, however, at some point in their lives had become Christians, though they were secretive about their new faith. At that time, in that environment, it was dangerous to be a believer; becoming a Christian would disgrace your family.

Oddly enough, both these women, living in two separate small villages miles and miles away from each other, had each become believers in Jesus. Neither hid her new belief from her children, though did so from everyone else. While most of their offspring went back to practicing Hinduism when they married, my dad and mom, independently and alone of all their many brothers and sisters, had developed a strong Christian faith along the way.

My parents were married in a Hindu ceremony, of course, conducted by a Hindu priest, who officiated at the most auspicious time according to Hindu astrology. My mom had never been shy about professing her faith but on this occasion, she held her tongue. She has been threatened and knew better than to disgrace her family.

So, she didn't say anything about her beliefs before the wedding; neither did my dad in the limited time they spent together.

Incredibly, they married without either knowing this big secret about the other. On their honeymoon, while my father was in the shower, my mother was sitting in their hotel room thinking all this over. "I don't even know this person," she thought. "What have I done?" She pulled out her Bible and leafed through it, seeking some comfort.

My dad suddenly came back into the room; she stood up and quickly tried to hide the Bible behind her back. "What are you hiding?" he asked.

"Nothing," she said.

"We cannot hide things from each other," my dad told her. Reluctantly, she showed him what was in her hands.

"Praise God!" he proclaimed, the moment he realized what she was holding. My parents realized that amazingly, they shared the same non-Hindu faith. The odds of this happening in an arranged marriage in India at that time were less than miniscule. It was unheard of, a miracle. This was a true sign and the most promising beginning: they were meant to be. God had brought them together.

Those of Christian faith like me believe that God has a plan for each of us, which may or may not line up with the plans we make for ourselves. We can try, but we cannot always predict or plan every aspect of our lives.

While this isn't my own story, it's still one of my favorite to tell about my parents. They had led two completely separate lives. They had been strangers in every sense of the word, yet education, becoming a professional, and leaning into Christianity were incredibly important to each of them. My dad broke barriers created by his own parents to become educated and created a life bigger than anyone in that village could ever have imagined. My mom shattered her own barriers. She was a woman who became a doctor in a world where women were not traditionally educated and were exclusively homemakers. They were a perfect match in every sense of the word, and while it would all appear like happenstance on the surface, they truly were created for each other.

Reflection:

While my grandmother had a reach far beyond her own children and fueled multiple generations of doctors, my grandfather did as well. While he hoped that his son would develop a passion for the movie industry and stay and run the family business, films perhaps triggered a desire to want more in life and dream bigger.

Movies have always been a constant in Indian culture. The Indian movie industry that started more than a century ago parallels Hollywood with how grandiose it can be. Perhaps the movies provide an escape from the harsh realities of life in a country where poverty was and remains widespread. Or, in my opinion, it was what dreams were made of. Movies showed everyone, no matter what your life circumstances, there was something bigger and better out there. Something that is within your reach. I think this was perhaps why my dad had such huge dreams for himself at such a young age. He grew up working in his dad's theaters, feeding physical film reels into projectors for playback on the big screen. He saw how big the world was even though he was in such a tiny village in India.

My dad, for as long as I could remember, loved Indian cinema. I remember weekends growing up watching movies with him at home. I can't say I understood much, but as a kid, it was easy to get drawn in solely by the vibrancy of the colors, music, and beauty of the actresses. Maybe this was what planted the seed in me as a little girl. The confidence these actresses portrayed, and their unparalleled beauty was a force to be reckoned with as a young impressionable kid.

Indian Cinema (Bollywood) was perhaps my first introduction into beauty standards that I would revisit much later in life as a plastic surgeon. Though the desire to be considered "beautiful" by global standards is universal, and Indians definitely undergo plastic surgery in increasing numbers, there is one big cultural difference. Indian celebrities and women in general are far more private than their Hollywood and American counterparts. The expectation is for them to not only look ethereally beautiful and flawless, but naturally so. Same for my older Indian female patients. This is very much a private matter to be treated with the utmost discretion, which is understood, always respected and honored.

As an American surgeon, I've always found it an honor that my Indian patients feel a level of comfort with me that they wouldn't otherwise. This also provides me with a unique understanding and ability to inspire young medical students in India to consider plastic surgery as their path.

Chapter Two

The Making of My American Family

My newlywed parents arrived in America and hustled, the way immigrants have always done and still do.

After their brief honeymoon in India my dad flew back to the United States, and my mom followed several months later once her visa was finally approved. As soon as her plane touched down, it was time to get to work. She began the process of studying for her US medical exams. As with all foreign medical graduates, she had to pass several qualifying and licensing exams in the United States in order to proceed with her training. This took a few years. Once this process was completed, she had to focus her attention on getting into a residency program. In the meantime, I came along. It wasn't ideal timing. She and my dad were focused on building. Building a life, a career, a path. Now, a family, too.

While I would spend endless weeks and months during my own medical school years trying to figure out which specialty I wanted to pursue, my mom did not have that luxury. She had numerous interests—she loved psychiatry, for example—but for her, the decision was more practical. Which residency program could she find that was driving distance from home and was somewhat conducive to her being a new mother? She wound up finding an excellent residency in pediatrics. Her original plan was to do a concentrated specialization in that area—which would give her advanced training—but then my brother arrived. Again, not the best timing. Mom now had an infant and a four-year-old to care for; the time and logistics needed to further her specialization became prohibitive. She decided to practice as a general pediatrician.

Reflection:

I was an adult and already a surgeon before I truly understood the extent to which my mom sacrificed her career for her family. My parents created lives for my brother and me where we never had to sacrifice our own goals. They ensured that neither of us would ever have to worry about taking out student loans or working jobs to finance our education. In medical school, the only thing I had to worry about was doing well so that I could pursue whatever specialty I wanted. I spent months thinking about what I wanted to do.

I didn't have to sacrifice any of my professional goals due to family or financial responsibilities like my mom had. I focused on my career goals. I had always thought when I had achieved what I wanted in my career, my personal desires and aspirations would just fall into place. But there's always a give and take: you must sacrifice in one area to achieve in another. While it's nice to think that we can do it all. It's just not possible. Indra Nooyi, the former CEO of PepsiCo, once famously stated that women cannot have it all. They cannot give 100 percent at work and 100 percent at home. There will always be a give and take and different seasons of life.

At the time, my father was working as a pharmacist and even joined with some friends to open their own pharmacy. Unfortunately, mixing friends and business doesn't always end well, which was exactly the case for my dad. The day he walked away from that business venture was the day he made a resolution to never work for or with anyone again. He would be his own boss. With my mom now done with her residency, it was the perfect time to open a pharmacy with a medical practice next door.

My parents officially worked together side by side in New York City. Their first location was in The Bronx; it was called JR Smita Pharmacy ("J" was for Jesus and "R" for Ramanadham). In the following years, they opened several other pharmacies, but eventually closed them due to pressures from the mafia and multiple threats and attempted robberies for narcotics. They eventually made the move to Washington Heights where they opened Mahesh Pharmacy (named after my brother). It's quite a gentrified area these days, but back in the 1980s it was not. Both my parents were held up at gunpoint in their businesses on multiple occasions, but this never deterred them, at least not from this location. They always showed up for work.

They worked long hours, and with hard work, their businesses excelled. It was a different time in medicine, when independent medical practices and one-man operations could succeed with ease. Both my parents were highly driven to succeed, but they also didn't have a choice. With young children and no local family support, failure was not an option. The most important part of my dad's original dream was coming true: he and my mom were creating a life in which his children could have all of the opportunities he did not.

Reflection:

My father had been a low-level employee making very little money when he first arrived in New Jersey, but he was always working toward a goal: creating the job and work he wanted. His first entrepreneurial venture with friends did not work out, but that did not deter him. He and my mother dived into their own businesses side by side, united and never at the mercy of anyone else's whims. If they were unhappy or unfulfilled, they could change that. These were the upsides. However, solo business owners bear all the responsibility and risk. Ultimately, they did not have any other choice but to sacrifice and work hard, as success was the only option. There was too much to lose if they failed.

As with any path, there are upsides and downsides; you can choose your own option. While my parents took this path to build a future for us in America, it came with sacrifices—their health, travel, and, more important, time with us. They spent most of our childhood away from home, building their businesses so that we wouldn't have the struggles they had. As an adult, I look back on everything they provided for us with awe and appreciation. We never had a worry in the world, because they took on this burden. Most of all, no matter what the sacrifices were, we knew that we were completely loved by them and were their world.

Just about the time my brother was born, my parents bought a house in suburban New Jersey. They had zero desire to raise a family in the city, given the crime, drugs, and hassles of NYC back in the 1980s. They wanted to raise their children in a quieter, calmer, and safer environment. It was a far-from-ideal commute for my parents, driving in and out of Manhattan every day with all the other commuters, but the trade-off—a safe neighborhood for us to run around in and good public schools—was well worth it to them.

The town that I grew up in was fairly diverse; there were many Asian families and a large Jewish population. A number of other Indian families were around, but those kids were not in the local public school with me. In fact, I don't remember even seeing other Indian students in elementary school. There were other Asian children, but no other Indians.

I was a classic first-generation kid who wanted nothing more than to integrate into the macro culture. I remember my intense desire to leave my Indian culture behind when I entered grade school. My parents were doing their best to navigate their new country and make a success of their own small businesses. In tandem, they did their best to raise us in a world that didn't follow the same cultural norms or values they knew growing up. I went to public school wanting only to fit in with my classmates. There were some bumps along the way, as my home life was quite different from that of most of my classmates.

India remained very much a part of our lives in my early years. We traveled there frequently, but never together as an entire family. One of my parents always needed to stay behind to manage the growing businesses, especially in the early years. I do have fond memories of visiting my family in India; we had a large extended family there with plenty of cousins, aunts, and uncles. We stayed with them, wore Indian clothing, and put fresh jasmine in our hair. It was a time when my parents looked relaxed and happy—they were home after all! This was very different from growing up in New Jersey where it was just the four of us.

My parents did not have significant help in the childcare department during our younger years. They went through many nannies that all turned out to be untrustworthy, relied on friends or late daycare pickups which also proved to be unreliable due to their workload and late commutes back in from the city. They eventually convinced my grandparents to alternate coming to New Jersey to stay with us once my brother and I were in elementary school. My dad's mom (Grandma) and mom's dad (Thatha) would come to live in our house for six months at a time, then return to India while the other grandparent took their six-month turn. In Indian culture, elders are highly respected; it is not unusual for parents and grandparents to live at home with their kids and grandkids. Mine served an essential function: watching over my brother and me. Our parents worked long hours in the city; they never returned home before six or seven in the evening. Our grandparents were there to care for us after school and give us dinner if my parents were delayed.

My brother and I didn't speak much Telugu anymore. I was fluent when I was young but in kindergarten, I would mix up my English and Telugu together and my teachers eventually told my parents to stop speaking to me in Telugu at home. While I still understood it, I couldn't speak it at all. My brother understood even less but learned to "figure it out." We certainly couldn't communicate well with my grandparents. This, to this day, remains one of my biggest regrets, and perhaps one I blame my parents for. We couldn't really speak with them, short one-word responses from us in English didn't really set the stage for meaningful relationships, but we loved them, nonetheless, and were heartbroken when they passed away years later.

Looking back, probably the hardest part of this arrangement for them was the lack of the sociable culture in the United States. In India, doors were always open, neighbors and family were always walking around and popping in and out of others' homes, where multiple generations lived under one roof. Everyone was often outside, visible. While my grandparents loved being with us, living in our insular American suburb was tough on them. They were always definitely ready to get back to India when their time with us was up.

While we were alone in many ways, our home was always open to anyone visiting from India, meaning we often had a full house. Friends and family came to stay for weeks at a time. Some of these were just social visits and some were lengthy as these families would stay at our home while they saved money or made definitive arrangements for their own move to America. My parents always had their doors open, their refrigerators full, and fresh food on the table for anyone who needed their help. They would make time for anyone even though they were incredibly busy themselves.

While I wanted to assimilate as best as I could with my American friends and the American way of life, my parents were also trying to maintain our Indian culture and raise us the same way they were raised. Therefore, we were very much a traditional Indian family behind the closed doors of our home.

My mother lovingly put coconut oil in my hair every night to make it smooth and shiny; that's just what Indian moms do for their daughters. None of the other girls in school did that; this was years before it became cool and trendy as it is now to use argan or coconut oil for good hair health. We also had Indian food for dinner every night. The aromas would fill the house but also leave a lasting scent on all our clothing, even those that were fresh out of the dryer.

Playing sports was never stressed or encouraged; playing musical instruments was. We couldn't play with our friends unless our homework was done. Listening to Western music and going to concerts was also not allowed until we were much older. My parents did their best to instill good study skills and keep us focused on our education during our younger years. Looking back, I'm grateful for this, but at the time, these were just more rules that made us different from everyone else. And different was the last thing I wanted.

***

Looking back at that time, I never realized how torn we were between our Indian life at home and our American life at school. Because of this, I don't think I ever felt like I fit in. I didn't fit in with our Indian family friends, and I never really fit in with my friends at school, either. Perhaps this is why I was always a shy and timid kid. It was easier to just blend into the background than to stand out and be different.

My brother and I just had to find our own way and create the perfect mix of both cultures. This came into play more as young adults: in high school, college, and certainly for me in medical school. Ultimately, our Indian heritage was the biggest blessing. The things that I pushed aside when I was young are things that I embrace now. Indian culture is beautiful, it's colorful, it's unique. The clothing, jewelry, food, and just the eclectic beauty of Indian women is astounding. I wish I had spent more time learning our native language, studying traditional dances, or even watching Bollywood movies with my dad.

My dad more so than my mom loved all things Indian. He would buy Indian newspapers every week in Edison (the "Little India" of New Jersey) and watch Indian movies whenever he could. He didn't even get his American citizenship, because that meant he would have to give up his Indian citizenship. Now that he's gone, I'm even more interested in holding my culture tight. The things that made me different as a kid are what make me unique as an adult.

I only ever knew my mother as a doctor. From my earliest memories, she went out the door every day in her sari with a white medical jacket over it and headed off to the city with my dad, usually six days a week. I spent much more time with Dad as a child because he could at least take me to work with him if they didn't have childcare. My mom for the first years of my life was a resident, so she was around less.

In her practice, Mom treated a diverse group of mostly low-income patients, many on Medicaid with limited funds. She quickly learned to speak fluent Spanish because she had to; the neighborhood was predominantly Dominican Republican at that time. Mom fostered a warm connection with her patients. Seeing how much of an impact she had on their lives stirred my early desire to want to become a doctor. It was also what made it OK in my eyes that she wasn't home for us much as kids. We never had the mom who had snacks waiting for us when we came home from school or did pick-ups and drop-offs. Looking back at that time, that was what I missed most—but I saw with my own eyes how she brought light and comfort into many difficult situations. For this, I felt like the sacrifice of time with my mom was worth it, as she was helping so many.

Though she was a pediatrician, soon enough she started doing everything for everyone, of all ages. This was in the days before "urgent care" facilities on every corner, so in a sense that was how she functioned. Because so few other doctors were available nearby, she gradually wound up seeing everyone in the family. First the babies and kids, then their parents, grandparents, and friends. Pretty much every local eventually passed through her clinic.

When we came through the door of her clinic we would be greeted by a packed waiting room, a crowd of people anxiously sitting there needing to see her. The clinic also accepted walk-ins, sometimes really urgent matters, so it could get quite crowded with long waiting times. As soon as she walked in, the mood in the room changed; all the patients visibly brightened and calmed down at the sight of her. Mom had great rapport with all of them; she had become an integral part of the community. I particularly noticed that the patients always seemed to come out of the consultation room smiling, already feeling better and reassured. I also appreciated that while she might not always have been home for my brother and me, she was doing a lot of good in the world.

Not that it came easy. What affected her the most deeply were the times she had to report incidents of child abuse to Child Protective Services. There were times she became suspicious when she saw certain injuries on young patients, and it was her legal and moral duty to report her findings to the authorities.

This process could become quite fraught; Mom had to make sure she and her staff were safe and protected from angry family members, and such incidents always weighed heavily on her. Not so much the reporting and any blowback she might face, but just seeing kids in that condition. She wanted every kid to have a safe and good family life—the type of life my parents were doing everything in their power to give my brother and me.

***

Middle school was particularly tough on me; that's certainly the time when adolescent kids can get mean. My best friends throughout elementary school no longer wanted to be friends with me. This seemed to happen literally overnight. It always felt like it had to do with the coconut oil in my hair, that I of course, began to refuse, or the lingering smell of Indian food on my clothes, but most likely it was just because I was different. My hair and skin color were different and at that age, being different is just plain weird. Regardless, whatever the case was, I found myself not having a core friend group and not feeling like I could relate to anyone.

I eventually realized that I would have to make an entirely new group of friends, which started with one Indian friend (who is still one of my closest friends to this day) and from there formed a small tight group. I felt confident heading toward high school because I had managed to find "my people." I was all set. Then my parents dropped a bomb; they announced that they were sending me to private school. Of course, I still had to take the exams to get in—which I actually considered failing on purpose—but I knew better. Regardless, I was not happy; they were ruining my life.

My brother had been having a tough time in the grade school I also attended. He was very distracted by his friends, and his grades were suffering. My parents felt he was being treated differently than the other boys in his class, possibly because of his skin color. Whatever the case, they wanted him out of the public school system and decided I should switch schools at the same time.

The new private school was located in our own town; it was academically superb and offered bussing to anybody who needed it. My parents would no longer have to worry about schedules and rushing back and forth in NYC traffic. This was a huge relief for them, but more importantly, they believed they were setting us up for academic success. For that, they would pay any price and make any sacrifice.

Reflection:

We all break barriers in our lives—and if we don't, we should! Whether they're barriers created by our own family and parents, social and cultural expectations or even limitations created by ourselves (the "I can't do this" mentality)—the only way to have a life fulfilled or one that you are proud of is to break the mold and push the boundaries.

In medicine, women have broken barriers for centuries. We certainly have come a long way from the nineteenth century when women were considered too weak to study and people believed that menstruation caused "temporary insanity" (Horatio Storer, MD—a Harvard-trained OB-GYN). Now, the number of female medical students surpasses male students. Studies even show that patients treated by female physicians have lower mortality rates and hospital readmission rates than their male counterparts. (JAMA, May 17, 2024.)

The history of how we got here is fascinating. The first US medical school for women opened in 1848 with a focus on attending to women during childbirth—because it was "unnatural" for men to attend to women during this time. Between 1850 and 1895, twenty more medical schools for women opened due to the newfound feminist movement. Elizabeth Blackwell was the first woman to graduate from a US medical school (accepted only because her application was thought to be a prank) and soon paved the way for all of us that followed.

In 1915, the first medical association for women was founded in the 1940s, women began to serve as physicians in the US military. By the 1970s, Congress passed the Title IX Education Amendment that prohibited federally funded schools from discriminating based on gender. A second wave of feminism resulted in dramatic changes, and in just a decade, between 1970 and 1980, more than 20,000 women graduated from medical schools, an enormous increase from only a decade before in 1960. Fast forward to 2017, when in the first time in history, women entering US medical schools outnumbered men. This has continued year after year.

We see this trend in surgery as well. The first female born doctor in Britain to earn a medical degree posed as a man until her death. Margaret Ann Bulkley (Dr. James Barry as she was professionally known, as a military surgeon in the British army) rose to become the Inspector General of Hospitals, serving across the British Empire and performed the first successful

C-section in South Africa. Dr. Bertha Van Hoosen was the first female surgeon admitted to the American College of Surgeons in 1913. In 1950, Dr. Kathryn Stephenson was the first woman to be board-certified as a plastic surgeon. In 1981, women comprised 1.4 percent of active general surgeons. Recent data shows that approximately 45.2 percent of general surgery residency positions in the US are held by women.

Women who break barriers open the doors for others. It's our responsibility to do that not only for ourselves but for younger generations. While we have come a far way, there's still more work to be done.

Chapter Three

Planning the Future: Start Early!

Given my Indian upbringing, I knew my job. It had been spelled out to me early on. "Just like we go to work every day, you go to school every day. Your job is to get good grades." It goes without saying that academic achievements were a priority at my house. Athletics and more "American" pastimes, not so much. My parents would have been okay with sports, had I truly been serious about pursuing one, but spare time was for learning to play instruments (by instruments I mean piano and violin), volunteering, and ongoing studying.

The makeup of my new private high school was varied, with students from every kind of background, including many other Indian students. So, it was four years of studying and volunteering, which was fine with me as I was highly focused on getting into a good college with a strong pre-med program. The hard work paid off as I made it into the Minuteman Society, an association, named after our mascot, of the top 10 percent of seniors academically, although this was never outrightly stated.

Our school required everyone to play at least one sport, so I signed up for volleyball as a freshman along with some friends. I played on the team for all four years, but it certainly wasn't my passion. The school also required that we all do a certain amount of volunteer work each year. So, during the summer, I volunteered as a candy striper at a local hospital. I also realized this would be helpful for my college and pre-med applications. The summer-school culture at my high school was strong, so many of us spent our summers taking classes and getting through our summer reading lists so that when the academic year formally began, we could be placed into the more demanding AP (Advanced Placement) and IB (International Baccalaureate) classes.

This is not to say that I never had any fun. I was serious about my grades, but I had a core group of high school friends and would spend weekends hanging out in the city, a short train ride away, shopping, or just hanging out at home. My parents typically gave us autonomy and flexibility with what and who we did things with as long as we maintained good grades. And by good, I mean straight A's.

Growing up it had never even been a question. *You're going to be a doctor.* So, as a junior in high school I was quite surprised to be officially summoned to the family living room one night. "We need to talk to you," my parents announced. I sat down nervously, wondering why they were being so weird and serious. What could I have possibly done?

"We want to talk about your future. What do you want to study in college and beyond?"

I was surprised. I hadn't realized I even had much choice in the matter. I'd been hearing one thing and one thing only, my entire life: *medicine.* "I thought medicine was what you wanted me to do?" I questioned.

My mother, a pediatrician, was seeing her practice upended by the recent upheaval in health maintenance organizations (HMOs). "This is all just starting, and it's going to get worse," she explained. "By the time you make it through medical school and are ready to start practicing, who knows what the landscape will look like? So we think you should reconsider medicine and start thinking about pharmacy," she proclaimed along with my dad. At this point, my dad had a booming generic pharmaceutical manufacturing company in New Jersey. My parents' plan was for me to go to pharmacy school and then learn the business from my father.

Now I was truly surprised. But at this point, I really did want to become a doctor. Pharmacy was not of any interest to me whatsoever. I was able to convince my parents to let me pursue my medical dreams with the promise that one of two things would happen: I would either not do a residency after medical school, or I would do a short three-year residency, and then come home to learn the business.

That was where we left my future for the moment.

Healthcare was undergoing a sea change; big chain stores like Wal-Mart and Walgreens were opening in-store retail pharmacies or offering competitive pricing that was impossible to match as an independent small pharmacy. Dad had seen the writing on the wall. Though he had practiced in retail pharmacy, his dream was always to do more, to manufacture. In fact, he spent many years when I was a child taking evening classes and working towards his Doctorate in Pharmacy degree at Long Island University in Brooklyn. 1990 turned out to be the perfect time to go for his dreams, he opened his very own generic manufacturing company.

While he had a team of chemists, other pharmacists, R&D guys, a packaging department, and whoever else was needed to make a medication from formulation to packaging, he still oversaw, approved, and double- and triple-checked everything. In fact, oftentimes, it was his own formulations that eventually passed the grueling testing process. Regardless, he was forced to wear many hats along the way; I was impressed by his business-savvy skill set. I inherited his childhood desire to be a surgeon, absolutely, but did not possess his entrepreneurial genes, or so I thought.

He had eventually built his business into a successful company. My dad now had the satisfaction of seeing many of his own "new" drugs come to life in the marketplace as generic brands which were widely prescribed to patients at a much more affordable price. He created a wide variety of medications including antihistamines, antimuscarinics, analgesics, narcotics, and cardiac medications. This meant his reach was far. He played a large role in healing and relieving symptoms for anyone with allergies or pain to patients with pulmonary, urinary, or cardiac disease, and more. It was inspiring to see him create and fulfill a lifelong dream. He could have been a surgeon, treating one patient at a time, if he had his own way, but God had bigger plans for him. He was able to treat thousands of people who benefited from taking the medications he created.

***

Once my dad's business was well-established, my mom took a good look around her own clinic and realized things weren't quite the same there either. She and her staff were getting harassed by patients all the time as a narcotics wave swept the country.

Oxycontin addiction was out of control in her neighborhood. Passersby would see the words "Doctor" or "Clinic" on her sign, come rushing into her office, and demand drugs. They would frequently threaten staff and my mom, who would refuse to write a prescription for painkillers on the spot. That on its own wouldn't have been enough to deter her, but the whole medical landscape was changing so fast, as well. Mom was no longer getting reimbursed by insurance companies for services she had rendered without endless hassles and red tape to combat.

As I was preparing to apply to college, it really struck my mom that I would soon be gone, and that she had missed a great deal of my childhood and adolescence. It was time she could never get back. My brother still had a few more years left at home, so she decided to be more present for him. This was what pushed her to make her own big life change: she effectively retired from her own practice. Mom could now go to work with my dad if she felt like it, and help whenever it was needed. She could stop by in the middle of the day to bring him lunch, run over anytime with something he forgot at home, or bring a special smoothie as a treat. She would oversee the other employees and brainstorm ideas with my dad. They always seemed to talk shop at dinner, as a result. They were their own little team working hard to make the business successful.

However, my mother did not give up medicine altogether. She could never do that. Medicine was her passion. She would regularly fill in for her doctor friends if they were vacationing or traveling. Mom was an accomplished woman who had run her own successful practice for many years, but at her core, she was still a traditional Indian wife and mother.

Reflection:

It's funny how influential your parents or whomever you surround yourself with can be without you even realizing it. My dad wanted more out of life. He saw an opportunity to achieve bigger and better things and figured out how to make it happen. Similarly, my mom never worked for anyone. She practiced medicine on her own terms. She had autonomy.

My parents worked hard, but as long-term entrepreneurs, they remained flexible. When they saw which way the wind was blowing in terms of independent pharmacies and small medical practices, they adjusted. The landscape of their long-time businesses they had put so much into was changing; they rolled with the punches and were willing to change course.

These were excellent lessons for me to absorb. There is nothing better than being your own boss. Working for myself was never something I had even remotely thought about. But a day would come when I had to take matters into my own hands—just like my dad did. Hard work was something I was never afraid of. Being unfulfilled, however, was something I just couldn't live with. I didn't realize how big of an impact their decisions had made on me until I was standing in their shoes a couple of decades later.

Flexibility is crucial for a successful business. The market, the consumer, the environment change—and priorities change with that. Patients change, their goals change, and their priorities and lifestyle change as well. As physicians, it's important to meet patients where they are, and flexibility in business keeps that business relevant and competitive.

My parents were no longer commuting every day into New York City, but I had my heart set on going to college there, specifically, to Columbia University. While some schools had their own application or supplemental applications, many colleges accepted one common application. I was waiting outside my guidance counselor's office on the day we lined up to turn in all our paperwork. I started chatting casually with my best friend at the time about which schools we were applying to. I looked at her list; she looked at mine. "Tufts?" I asked, noticing she had checked that box.

Instinctively and on the spot, not even thinking about it, I checked one more box, the one for Tufts, so my application would be submitted there along with my records. I did this on a whim; it was another safety school I could have as a backup. Columbia was all I was thinking about, however. In all my applications, I had checked off pre-medicine as what I wanted to study. It was my honest answer. I did not realize at that time—nor did my counselor—that this was not the savviest strategy.

Given that I was Indian, expressing this desire was probably the worst thing I could do in terms of getting admitted to my college of choice. Columbia was not looking for another Indian pre-med student; the university, like many others, had an overabundance of similar applicants. In the end, I did not get into my top choice. I was offered a place at a number of other schools, Tufts being one of them.

Top of my mind was one concern: what's the long-term plan to get into a top medical school? I certainly had no intention of going out of the country for medical training—that was out. Medical schools were getting more selective by the year, so where should I go for undergrad? Which college would be my best bet? I considered every possibility. If for some reason I did not get into medical school, what was my backup plan going to be? "Go to business school instead," I decided.

Tufts, a prestigious liberal arts college, had an excellent medical school and its own affiliated hospital, New England Medical Center (now Tufts Medical Center). Tufts did not have a business school or a business major, but it was located in Boston. I had decided I didn't want to be in New York City if I couldn't be at Columbia, and two of my closest friends from high school were also going to Tufts. If I did, too, I'd be in a fun city with them, and had planned out a backup if medical school didn't work out. I would get a solid economics degree and head for business school. This was how I gamed everything out—my master plan as a senior in high school. It seemed like the best workable plan, and Tufts it was.

***

So, off I went to college life in Medford, Massachusetts. My parents dropped me off at the dorm on the first day of pre-orientation. I, along with my friends from high school, had been invited to the international orientation, which all the other international students also attended. I was so glad to have made the effort to go, because some of the friendships I made those first few days would eventually turn out to be very influential for my future path.

The best thing about my first couple of years away from home was how I really came out of my shell. While my parents had been quite flexible in what we were allowed to do as long as our grades did not suffer, college was still a time when I learned more about myself, as many college students do. I had new friends from different backgrounds and upbringings. I had many friends, different groups of friends. I lived in the dorms my first two years quite happily and embraced college life.

I was carrying a heavy academic load as an economics major with an art history minor on top of all my pre-med requirements. Nothing overlapped. This actually worked out well because it exposed me to such a wide group of friends and I took advantage of everything a liberal arts school could offer.

Tufts offered an accelerated program for pre-med students. Sophomores had the opportunity to apply to Tufts medical school early to reserve a guaranteed space in their program. I did not do that; I was thinking at the time that I wanted to return to New York for medical school. I didn't want to be locked down into anything. But for the time being, I needed to firm up a place to live for my last two years of college.

Housing was not guaranteed at Tufts after freshman and sophomore years. A few of us, including my sophomore-year roommate, found a house to rent. It was a six-bedroom house that we turned into an eight-person house. We wound up with eight young women, some of whom were completely random friends of friends. While it got crowded and crazy at times, it was the beginning of some lifelong friendships.

My study schedule was punishing, but the bonds I forged in that house have lasted until today. Five of us remain the tightest of friends, even after life has taken us to very different places. We had so much fun just doing what college girls do. These were the girls I lived with, shared a bathroom with, drank with, went out dancing and clubbing with, had long talks about boyfriends and intense discussions about our futures. They were my best friends and remain a blessing. I have no doubt that these bonds will last a lifetime.

Reflection:

Thinking back on my younger years, I truly do not think I could have gotten through all the ups and downs and challenges life throws your way without my friends, who became like sisters. These ladies were ultimately my cheerleaders, my biggest support system. There was recently a long-term generation Harvard study published that looked at key factors that contribute to longevity. When I first heard about this, of course, as a doctor, I assumed it would be the usual healthy eating, exercise, no smoking, no alcohol. To my ultimate surprise, the key to a long life well lived is your relationships. Strong social connections result in a longer, healthier, life with less mental and physical decline. So, keep that group tight. Don't take friendships lightly. Be selective. Be picky. Invest in those friendships. You're ultimately investing in yourself by doing so. This creates an environment that will undoubtedly motivate you to be more successful. This is not only important for yourself but for those who inspire you. If your mentors are pushed to their fullest, so are you. You in turn can do the same for your own mentees. The benefits are endless.

With junior year came another big, standardized test. In fact, the MCAT (Medical College Admission Test) was a big, big deal. I was so nervous about it that the thought of studying abroad, which all of my friends did that year, was not even an option. To this day, foregoing this experience is still one of my biggest regrets. In any event, at the end of my junior year of college I took the MCAT and did well. I took it again because one can always do better and medical schools typically take the best score.

Medical school is very different from college in terms of admissions. I got into several schools in the Northeast including some programs in Boston. But after going to interviews and getting a sense of the culture at each of these schools, it seemed that staying at Tufts was the right choice for me.

Med school can be a cutthroat, competitive environment. Students seek every advantage; those in the same program are competitive even with each other and undermine one another, seeking to make their peers look bad. All so they can shine brighter. That simply wasn't my way or an environment I wanted to be in, though I saw a lot of that at other schools I visited, too. Tufts Medical was a bit of an anomaly at that time; its leaders truly wanted every one of its students to succeed. The sort of backbiting environment I was seeing elsewhere was frowned upon there.

Reflection:

I never quite understood the whole undermining backstabbing culture that medicine often promotes; a culture often seen in any competitive field. The effort, drama, and stress that comes from constantly looking at what others are doing is wasteful and transparent. I already had the philosophy of only controlling what you can control, and that's yourself. Put your head down, work hard, and be the best that you can be. Anyone watching you (let's be frank, you are always being watched in these settings) will see your effort. They'll see that you are honest, hard-working, a team player, and just get things done. That's who they want and who you should want to be. This sentiment spans all professions and certainly something I look at now that I'm on the other side. With my staff, with residents, hard work will always shine brighter than trying to look better at the cost of someone else. This ultimately only creates a toxic environment where no one is living up to their true potential.

So, for med school I only moved across town—from the suburbs of Boston to the medical school campus in the heart of the city, where I would stay for the next four years. But before I cracked my first book open, I made one momentous trip to India—this time with my entire family! My cousin, the daughter of the uncle whose home we always stayed in while visiting, was getting married. She was a food engineer, and her intended husband was a businessman. This was an excellent match; everyone concerned was pleased with this union. It also happened to be the first big family wedding of which I was a part of. The elaborate celebration, with multiple days of ceremonies and parties, was a can't-miss event.

I was frantically busy with a summer job in a science lab, so my brother and mom arrived first. The minute I could get away, Dad and I flew to India and joined everyone at my uncle's familiar house, the scene of many happy childhood memories. Staying there put us very much in the center of everything.

Day after day (and night after night) we dressed up in our finest and went out for celebratory events. The entire wedding revolved around Hindu culture, so each day there was a new festivity to attend, like the Puja, a ceremonial worship ritual that takes place before the marriage.

This elaborate wedding was truly a joyous occasion. I was thrilled to be part of the big whirlwind. All eyes were on the bride, but I was under my own small spotlight, as well. Many thought I'd be the next one to get married as I was now nearing age twenty. Fortunately, as a junior in college I was still a bit young for such serious scrutiny. So, I didn't pay it any mind. I was going to be a doctor. It was time for the next big step: medical school.

Reflection:

Looking back on my years in college and medical school, I can honestly say it was one of the best times of my life. I became more confident and became more secure in my own skin. I formed solid friendships and professional relationships. I was focused on the next goal, always, but I enjoyed my life. My parents laid the groundwork for establishing a strong foundation, strong values, and a superior work ethic—but sometimes you just need to be on your own to really fly. This was the first time that I felt like I fit in. I didn't have to be "American" or "Indian," I could just be me. People either accepted me, or they didn't, and I was starting to realize it didn't matter. I had to accept myself—and that was a beautiful mixture of cultures. It was this realization that set the groundwork for my future success in medical school and next residency. Each is harder than the last. But with each phase in life, the goal is always to learn what you need so you can be successful in the next step and bring all the earned confidence with you so that you have a platform to propel from. At the core of this success is faith and confidence in yourself, which sometimes is something you have learn over time.

Chapter Four

A Doctor Is Born

During my first week of medical school, an older student pulled a few of us aside to offer some unsolicited yet friendly advice. He said, "You'll have to study more than you ever have before, and you'll never be able to catch up on sleep so you might as well go out and have fun. We work hard and play hard here." These were wise words to live by as my class dived into schooling at a whole new level of intensity. The sheer volume of information we were expected to absorb in four short years was overwhelming. I knew that I'd worked hard during college, at what I thought was my peak capacity. But the degree of difficulty in medical school courses demanded a whole new level of focus and commitment.

When not at lectures, we were studying, reading, and poring over our notes. All the time. We tried to make it fun by studying with each other. We made studying a social event, making the best of a grueling situation. Our tests were clustered within a single week. We would repeat the pattern of studying endlessly for two to three weeks, followed by back to back exams throughout the first two years of school. The only way to get through this grueling schedule was to have something to look forward to, so we planned our nights out in the city weeks in advance. The one free night we gave ourselves was the night of our last exam. We would plan our nights to the T, shopping for something to wear that night, dinner, then getting ready.

The first two years of medical school were mostly spent in the classroom. But the workload and amount of knowledge we had to acquire in a short period was nothing we had ever attempted before. We learned microbiology, pharmacology, biochemistry, anatomy, physiology, histology, genetics, and more. The subjects were endless and wide-ranging. The only "hands on" learning we did was in the anatomy lab, where we dissected cadavers to better learn about human anatomy.

Reflection:

I had gone into medical school with the thought that I would become an infectious disease doctor. Maybe it was my fascination with the rare outbreaks that were occurring around the world that made me think I would work at the Center for Disease Control, eventually. But it was my first year of medical school, during anatomy, that I realized I loved using my hands. I loved the intricacy, complexity, and beauty of the human body. It started with the eyes, and subsequently I went through my first two years of medical school thinking I would become an ophthalmologist. The lesson I learned here, which would show up laced throughout my life, is to accept change. We all change, as do our desires. We learn more, we experience new things, we change course, and redirect. The one constant in life is change.

Third-year medical students begin doing clinical rotations, so as I entered my third year, I was finally able to spend time in the hospital. The purpose is to give students exposure to the bigger fields in medicine. By the end of the third year, most students would figure out where their passions lay and the areas where their skills and interests naturally intersected. During the fourth year, clinical rotations continued but students concentrated on their chosen subspecialty.

Some of us knew the direction we wanted to go and had been laboring since year one with the underlying goal of obtaining our desired residency. If we were not completely sure or if it had changed, which was what most commonly happened, we had to do our best to avoid any shut doors or lost opportunities.

Testing was continual. The first big test, which would determine which specialties we had a chance of getting into, was the United States Medical Licensing exam (USMLE) Step 1. There were, at the time, three Step exams during medical school and a fourth and final test during residency. Step 1 was and is the most important of all the exams. This tests all your basic science knowledge—everything you learned during the first two years of medical school. At the time, you had to score at least a 200 to even be considered for a surgical residency of any kind. The point was to weed out those less likely to succeed. The pressure was unrelenting to score well enough on every test and move on to the next step. And, at the same time, to be present and alert.

The hierarchy in medical school is well-defined: the attending physician is at the top. The attending physician is the fully licensed and board-certified doctor, who has completed all of his or her training. We were helping in the care of their patients, but they are ultimately responsible. Residents, as doctors in training are called, report to the attending physician. Medical students are the lowest rung on the totem pole. Our job was not only to be present, observe, and learn along the way, but to make the residents' jobs easier. Every morning, we would arrive at the hospital before they did. Part of the daily morning routine was to collect information on all the patients we were caring for, including lab test results, results of studies performed, and how they were doing overall. A good student would run around and collect lab results and vital signs for the patients and share this information with our residents. It was one less thing they would have to do themselves. This was at the time that all vital signs would be written on a clipboard in their rooms, so we literally had to run around.

We would then go on walking rounds with them, meaning we would physically check and examine every patient. This included asking them how they were feeling and examining their surgical sites. To truly expedite this process, we would carry clean bandages, tape, and scissors with us and remove the patients' surgical dressings as they were talking to the residents. The residents then simply looked at the surgical site and left the room, moving on to the next patient. We students then quickly covered the wound or incision with fresh bandages and caught up with the team.

We asked questions so that we could learn, but we couldn't ask too many questions because that would be annoying. If we did our part well, blended into the background when needed or stepped up when appropriate, we were given the green light to do more. For example, to help suture or do minor procedures with the supervision of our residents.

Medical students had to be present and ready to help in any way while also being invisible. We couldn't get in the way of our residents or slow them down. We had to read the room, read the personality of the resident, and be as helpful as possible—and never leave until we were dismissed. This was where the human factor came into play. Clinical rotations in the third and fourth year were not only about learning the material and gaining hands-on experience, but also about getting along with the rest of the team and being able to work together as a unit.

Every day we would walk around and see patients with the attending physician and discuss their treatment plans. We call this "teaching rounds." During this time, the attending physician might ask a question. It might not even be related to a specific case. Sometimes the attending liked to toss out general questions out of the blue. "What's X disease, and how do you best treat it?" Or suddenly demand an answer to the most random anatomy question. If we happened to know the answer, we did not pipe up with it immediately—not unless we were directly asked. We'd go so far as to quickly scribble a helpful word or two on a note, maneuver behind the attending and try to show our resident the answer if he or she appeared to be stuck. They were sleep-deprived and spent all their time trying to keep patients alive and well cared for, so they had not always gotten around to reading about every single obscure disease and treatment.

Students did themselves no favors by trying to make themselves look good if doing so made a resident look bad. So much of our future lay in the residents' hands. They were the ones who were spending a great deal of time with us, observing us, helping us, and reporting to the attending on how well or poorly we performed. Attendings relied on these recommendations; they typically had very little face time with us other than in the OR (operating room). The amount of sway that residents held over the students is hard to overstate.

Probably one of the most important things during the third year of medical school is to gain an understanding of the atmosphere around each specific specialty. Every field has its own distinct personality. A plastic surgeon is very different from a neurosurgeon or pediatrician, for example. They're just different personalities, with different mindsets, goals, and ways of working. Not to mention lifestyles. We students were all looking to find our field, and much of that meant finding "our people." The ones we clicked with.

As a third-year medical student my first rotation was OB/GYN, and I loved every minute of it. I had such skilled residents overseeing me; they were helpful, encouraging, and fun. They allowed us to help with medical procedures, too. This was also my first experience in the operating room. I'll never forget when I made the rookie mistake of showing up on my first day without eating breakfast and not wearing supportive shoes, only to be delegated to the OR for a gynecological surgery where I had to hold retractors for what seemed like hours. Retractors are instruments used during surgery to provide exposure for the surgeon. You might be holding back skin, soft tissues or even organs. You had to hold it in place, perfectly still, using as much strength as needed without moving. Moving would mean the surgeon's view may be obstructed. At times, I remember my muscles quivering and burning in pain but trying my hardest to not shift or reposition. This simple task delegated to medical students or the most junior person in the room was never so simple.

My feet were killing me. It was also hot in a full gown, mask, and cap under the bright OR lights, and I began to feel dizzy. I wound up having to scrub out and drink juice and eat crackers. This was beyond embarrassing, but I quickly realized that I gained some "street cred" with the not-so-nice OR nurses, who, from that day on, were nice to me. It was a rite of passage. I finally caved and bought the not-so-fashionable Dansko shoes that most residents wore, and since then I've never shown up to the OR without having some food in my stomach.

The OR quickly became a place I loved. Treating pregnant women, delivering babies, and hanging out with these particular residents was fun and, of course, extremely rewarding. This group of doctors was so great that I decided that Obstetrics and Gynecology just might be my field, and I planned the rest of my year, and the fourth year, based on this feeling. I even applied for away rotations at other schools in OB/GYN.

Reflection:

The operating room isn't for everyone. In fact, people know quickly whether they love it or hate it. There is no in-between. It's all or nothing. What I experienced on my first day would most often deter students from a life in surgery. But for me, it opened me up to the culture of the OR. The surgeon is the lead in a well-orchestrated dance. Everyone has a unique role, but everyone is part of the team. Time went fast in the OR. It was fun and challenging. Sometimes in life you just know.

Part of this for me was that I could use my hands. Art was always part of my childhood. I sat in front of the TV watching Bob Ross and replicating his paintings when I was young; I took art classes on my summers off and during school. I loved using my hands to create something beautiful, whether it was a painting, drawing, or a piece of pottery. It was creative, expressive, and relaxing. The OR was no different. Using your hands to treat patient disease is beautiful and a true gift. Things seemed to be falling in place.

At that time, the field of OB/GYN was a really challenging specialty in medicine, mainly due to the schedule. If obstetrics was part of your practice, you had to be on-call and available at all times for your patients. You could easily be called in to the hospital night after night because your patients went into labor or had a complication that needed your urgent attention. It was a tough lifestyle, but that reality didn't deter me; I already knew that I loved surgery. I also loved my internal medicine rotation. So, OB/GYN seemed like a great mix of both surgery and medicine or clinical care. Luckily, change was in the horizon with the implementation of shift work and on-call coverage making the schedule more palatable. In the mid-late 2000's many practices were shifting so that doctors were only on call for twelve or twenty-four hour shifts. While this would mean that your personal OB may not actually be the doctor that delivers your baby when you go into labor, it led to better work hours, safety, and perhaps less physician burn out.

My first rotation in my fourth year was a maternal fetal medicine sub-internship. I wanted to make sure I liked the medical part of OB/GYN, the part that did not involve operating, but I realized this far more "medical" angle was not what I had imagined it would be. I found I was much less interested in the pregnancy process.

This sent me into a quick panic as I realized that as an OB/GYN, a significant portion of my career would involve this medical aspect which I did not like. I started meeting frequently with our dean, constantly talking over my options. "I love surgery, but I don't know if I like the lifestyle." Looking back this seems silly, because OB/GYN didn't offer a better lifestyle. But I had it in my head that surgery was much worse than OB/GYN. It was one additional year of training, four for OB/GYN instead of five for any surgical training. Change was also on the way in the field of OB/GYN with a push at the time toward shift work. That was not the case in surgery then. After spending the entire month of July in maternal fetal medicine, I realized I'd made a big mistake in choosing OB/GYN. Actually, I'd known this was not my path within days of starting that rotation.

My dean's advice was:

> In August, do a surgery rotation. You will know immediately if that's what you truly want to do, or not. You cannot make a career decision based on a five-year residency; you have to observe the attendings and see their lifestyle, not those of the residents. Whatever field you choose, you have to enjoy reading about it and constantly learning about it, because it's for life. If OB/GYN is not for you, then don't do it; but don't choose a field because of the lifestyle.

And therein lay the problem. I didn't have a female surgeon as a mentor or someone I looked up to. All the women that I came across who were surgeons were far from nice. They all seemed unhappy and miserable, and this often resulted in them being hostile to everyone around them. They were the very definition of why female surgeons get a bad rap. This was probably the first time in my life that I realized how important a role model and mentor was. Of course, I had my mom, but she wasn't a surgeon.

I took my dean's wise advice. And sure enough, on the very first day of my transplant surgery sub-internship, I was hooked. This was it; I had found it. I was going to become a surgeon. I loved using my hands to treat a patient's disease. I loved having a solution even if that solution was sometimes not to operate. I loved the personality of surgeons, their no-nonsense way of approaching things. They were straight shooters, made quick life-saving decisions, and took action. They also had fun, made jokes, and tried to make light of sometimes terrible situations.

Plastic surgery was always on my radar, and I had done a brief rotation in my fourth year of medical school, which really piqued my interest. I loved the surgeries, the art of it, and the plastic surgery personality which was a bit different than surgeons in general. While they encompassed all the traits mentioned above, there was also a unique attention to detail, finely-tuned intricate technical skills that necessitated being creative and having an artistic eye. The doctors I was learning from had fun, they truly loved what they did, there was diversity, this all seemed a bit different and better than what I had seen in general surgery. But, despite all of this, I wasn't sold on plastic surgery just yet. I wanted to save lives—that's why I went to medical school to begin with. At that time, I simply did not see plastic surgery as helping people in the way I would later come to appreciate. Plastic surgery procedures were fascinating and intricate and I was enthralled by every operation. But I was going to become a surgeon who saved lives.

***

While I was completely focused on my path in medicine and which field I would choose, at home something different was unfolding. First, I had to break the news to my dad that I wanted to do general surgery. This meant at least five more years of training. I would not be coming home to learn the family business. He, of course, knew me better than I knew myself, and I'd say a part of him was probably a little proud and excited that I planned to become the surgeon he'd wanted to be as a kid. I was also the daughter in the family. The load to carry on the family business and name fell on my brother's shoulders, as is typical in Indian households. I was off the hook.

At this point, I was now in my mid-twenties, and my family would have liked to see me married—soon. In a short time, I would be deemed "too old." When I shared my new plans with my parents, they were initially less than pleased. "You need to get married and settle down. What about raising a family?" Suddenly all the aunties and uncles were weighing in on my personal life. While my parents had always known that I was an artist at heart and surgery was now my passion, everyone else was very open about sharing their own opinions. Solicited or not.

It had been ingrained in my head from the time I was a kid: not only did I need to become a professional, I needed to marry a professional. Meaning a lawyer, a doctor, or a pharmacist. That was simply the Indian mentality, a given so obvious to immigrants from my parents' generation that it did not need to be stated aloud. My parents had other strong ideas about who might be "marriage material" for me, too. And surprisingly enough, being Indian was not at the top of their list.

That is not to say it didn't matter to them. When you are born to immigrant parents, they, of course, are concerned that the next generation will lose some of its heritage and the values they hold dear. Especially if their child marries outside the Indian race. I had spent the past three years of medical school being bombarded with introductions to potential suitors, every time I came home to visit. Every auntie, uncle, and friend of my parents came out of the woodwork to matchmake. It seemed that everyone had an eligible son or friend for me to meet. My parents were constantly introducing me to their friends' kids, who were mostly Indian. None of them led to any relationship, though. I simply was not interested. I was living my best life in Boston and was focused on my future.

I always kept my parents' words of wisdom in mind. When dating or considering a spouse, there were three crucial issues to consider. First and most important was *faith*: my parents and I shared a strong faith in God, and they strongly encouraged me to find someone with similar beliefs. This was by far the most important quality on their list. (One that would add an interesting wrinkle to the "Indian" consideration, as most Indians we knew were not Christian.) Next was *education*. My future husband needed to come from an educated family, and be equally educated as I was, if not more. Finally: *family*. Respect for elders is ingrained in Indian culture. Family gatherings play a big part in daily life, so anyone I was considering must be close to his own parents and siblings. "How they treat their own family is how they will treat you and your family," my father told me more than once.

At this juncture all such considerations were purely theoretical, because I wasn't getting married or even looking to be in a serious relationship. I wanted to become a surgeon, though I was getting a lot of pushback from my family. "It's just going to be so much work. You'll have zero personal life. You really want to become one of those mean overbearing female surgeons?" I had to reach deep inside myself to find enough confidence and trust in myself to follow my dream.

Which I did. Surgery was going to be my declared residency. Ironically enough, given all the chatter about marriage and family, my only priority was preparing for an entirely different kind of "match."

Reflection:

Saying "no" can be a superpower. It means that you value your own time, your values, your goals. But it can be one of the hardest words to articulate. To say no to that patient, to the parent, your friend, a mentor—the closer you are to that person and the more you respect him, the harder it is. But there is so much power in saying no.

It's easy to let other people influence your decisions. Everyone seems to have an opinion, but they are not living your life, they're not walking in your shoes, and they won't be dealing with the consequences of what that "yes" turns into. You'll only have yourself to blame.

This holds true in surgery, too, since once you touch a patient, you own her. You are responsible for her, for any possible bad outcomes or complications.

It took a while for me to learn how to say no. It's human nature to want to please. It's easy to say yes, but it's important to hold true to who you are and stick to your core values and beliefs. This comes with confidence and takes time.

Chapter Five

The Right Match

In their last year of medical school, all students apply for their residencies. This a binding contractual agreement made by a matching system. You send out your applications early in the academic year; you go to visit and interview at various programs, and all applicants rank their preference for every place they see. Meanwhile, the schools do the same thing on their end, picking a top choice of all the students they interviewed that runs down the list from No. 1 to dead last. All this data goes into a complicated computer algorithm, and each student winds up with a residency match. Now, it might be the school you chose last, but if that's where you matched, that's where you're going. Period.

A warning sign might come the Monday before the big announcement day, for any students who find out they didn't match anywhere. At that point faculty and deans swing into action; they start making calls and reaching out to see about open spots that may be available. They might point students in another direction: "You didn't get into any anesthesia programs, but there's an emergency medicine spot here," for example. But this is a small fraction of the members in each class. For the vast majority of medical students, their fate is sealed on National Match Day, held on the third Friday in March every year. It is an absolutely critical step on the long journey. A day of high expectations and much drama.

Naturally I had plotted and planned along with all my classmates for ages about our matches. I very much wanted to do my surgery residency at Mount Sinai in New York City—or anywhere in the city for that matter. I applied for several residencies elsewhere in NYC; I was determined to get back home. My mentor at Tufts, a general surgeon, was close friends with the chairman of the Mount Sinai program at the time. I had an excellent interview there; it honestly couldn't have gone any better. Mount Sinai also had a plastic surgery residency program and, of course, I had to make sure that I didn't close any doors just in case I decided plastic surgery was what I wanted to do. The chairman had been given the enthusiastic endorsement of my mentor, which often is what it takes to match with your No. 1 spot. I ranked Mount Sinai first and presumed it did the same for me, as I was told it did.

I had seen a number of impressive residency programs in my interviews. One interesting experience had been my time spent at the University of Texas Southwestern Medical Center. I had flown to Dallas and been wowed at what I saw there. It was immediately apparent that all surgeons in this program were at the top of their game. As I observed over my two-day stay, it was clear that I would have the skills and training to handle anything after going through their rigorous five-year residency. In short, UT Southwestern had an excellent program. But it was in Dallas, and that was less than desirable.

As I agonized over my rankings, I kept bumping it further and further down my list. In one of the many discussions with my father I told him that I didn't want to be in Dallas even if the program was great. And my parents *really* didn't want me living that far away for five years. "Then don't even put it on your list," he said.

"I can't leave it *off* my list, Dad, it's the best surgery program!" UT Southwestern did eventually go on my list but at No. 6, because Nos. 1 through 5 were all located in New York and in Chicago. The Top 5 choices on my part were purely location-based decisions. The distant No. 6 didn't worry me in the least. After all, I was set!

The big day arrived. In the long-standing tradition, one that has survived for generations, all the med school fourth-year students gather in one room, are handed their letters, and open them together right there on the spot. Many have family members in attendance because this ceremony is such a big deal. The culmination of years of study, preparation, and practice all comes down to this one match.

I opened my letter confidently. And saw the words in big black type: UT Southwestern. I was shocked. I was crushed, and I was far from alone. Some of my classmates were cheering and celebrating and hugging their family members, waving their letters in the air triumphantly. But there was also an immediate sizable exodus of devastated medical students rushing into the restrooms.

I, too, retreated to the bathroom, where many young women I knew were in there with me. Most of them walked in, entered a stall, and managed to shut and lock the door before bursting into audible tears and calling their family. By the time I got there, the bathroom was full of students similarly disappointed.

I found a spot along the wall and slid down, sitting on the floor. Immediately, I called my dad. I was crying and shocked that I would have to move to Dallas in a few short months. "I told you not to put Dallas on your list!" he said. But it was much too late for that.

After a few minutes I managed to pull myself together and return to the ceremony. I wandered around the room looking to find my friends and see where they were all going. "I'm moving to Dallas," I said to one of my closest friends.

"Wait, Dallas?" Someone else was going to Dallas and it turned out to be a long-time male friend, whom I had met long ago during international orientation at Tufts. We had a long journey together from college to med school, and he was like a brother. I frantically searched the room for him and raced up to him when I spotted him. We compared letters and sure enough, the same place: University of Texas Southwestern. An enormous feeling of relief swept over me. OK, a friend would be there too. And that was enough to get me through the emotional day.

I certainly had to readjust my plans. I was heading to Dallas, not New York City. In the days ahead I would come to terms with this alteration. As a Christian who believes in God, I once again was reminded that God has a path and a plan for each of us. How improbable that I should have landed in this particular place despite the most careful planning and so much advice and support from my mentors. Yet here I was.

As often happens with unanswered prayers, it would turn out to be the best possible match I could have made.

Reflection:

As I write this, I am reminded of how many times the unplanned, unexpected, and seemingly undesirable directions in which life took me worked out for the better. College was probably the first of these instances where I had made certain plans. I was confident I would get into my top school; I was at the top of my class with a GPA indicative of excelling in AP and IB classes; I had done well on my SATs. Not only was I confident, but my college guidance counselors were as well. Tufts was effectively my safety school. Life had other plans for me. God had other plans for me.

Fast forward to residency. Matching in my No. 6 spot was a true disappointment at the time. Seemingly any big plan I made for my future and life never seemed to work out, including in my personal life. And I'm grateful for that, looking back. The failed plans were, in fact, blessings. God had better plans for me. While, I was disappointed every time, I moved forward one day at a time and soon realized that I was in a better place because that original plan failed. It's always so important to be open to change, to shift your goals, and to reflect and appreciate where you are now and where you could have been. Life has a way of working out—but not without some bumps along the way.

A quotation that I love about this is from Mike Dooley, New York Times bestselling author : "Whenever something doesn't work out the way you thought it would, instead of thinking that something went wrong, see it as something that went unexpectedly well, but for reasons that are not yet apparent."

I had been in a series of bubbles my entire life: suburban childhood, college and medical school, always keeping my eye on the next goal. I had spent exactly zero time, aside from travel, outside the Northeast and its own distinct culture. The personalities are brusque, and people mind their own business; they walk fast and avoid eye contact with strangers. I'd spent so much time in Boston and New York, two big cities. I felt comfortable and fit in both places. I was about to hit real life in a very different way.

I was fully expecting a culture shock and did my best to prepare for Texas. I had some peace of mind and comfort knowing that I wouldn't be all alone there. I had my medical school friend and another from my college days, both of whom I surprisingly met at international orientation before college even formally started. So, I knew a total of two people. Two people with whom I was very close. It was definitely a start.

Many of the new residents who moved to Dallas bought condos or townhouses for the next five years of their lives; I wasn't about to commit to such a long-term arrangement. I was not at all sure how long I would last in Dallas. I was leaving myself an escape hatch, at least in my mind. I was more than ready to begin a surgery residency—for that part, I couldn't wait. But I was not ready for life in what was, to me, a foreign part of the country.

My brother and I drove my car—packed to the gills—down from New Jersey in pretty much one straight shot. We arrived in Dallas in less than a day and headed to my new apartment. I signed a one-year lease in a neighborhood called Uptown, with bars and restaurants and a quick ten to fifteen minute drive to the hospital. After a long day of unpacking and arranging, we needed a break and refueling. My brother and I decided to walk over to a local steakhouse just two blocks away. We didn't have the energy to search out and drive to someplace cool. On our short walks to and from the restaurant, we didn't see a single other pedestrian. I was accustomed to city life in Boston and New York, where you walked everywhere. This was quite the opposite and a big surprise. The first of many.

That weekend, my mom flew down to join us and help me finish settling in. My orientation was starting on Monday morning, and there was plenty of cleanup left to do. I was tired and feeling out of sorts; wearing sweats, I busily dumped and sorted and arranged. I made countless trips back and forth to the trash chute at the end of my hallway on Saturday morning to dispose of cut-up boxes and bubble wrap.

On one of my many trudges down the hall, a young woman, about my age, emerged from an apartment; our eyes met briefly as we passed each other. She was pretty and done up to a T. She wore cool jeans and a tight white tank top, heels, a full face of makeup, big blown out hair under a trendy hat, perfect nails, and lots of jewelry. She looked like she was heading out for a night on the town.

Twenty minutes later I was making yet another trip down the hall and saw the same girl coming down our shared hallway carrying a box of pizza. She returned to her apartment and shut the door behind her. She was that dressed up to go downstairs, cross the street, and pick up a pizza for lunch at home at 11 a.m. on a Saturday? This was something I had not seen before. My second surprise of the weekend. My sense of dislocation increased when I drove to some area stores for a basic stocking of the shelves.

Every person I encountered on these most basic errands, it seemed, had time to stop and have a conversation with me about anything and everything. If you made eye contact with someone, they were definitely stopping to say hello and start a conversation. I was not interested. I quickly moved on and was likely perceived as very rude. I was a Northeasterner after all. I had too much on my mind and on my plate to make small talk with random strangers, even if they were, indeed, the friendliest strangers I'd ever encountered. The social dynamics in the South were much different than what I was accustomed to. I just wanted to keep my head down and my mind focused. I was here for a purpose—to become the best surgeon I possibly could.

But even so, everyone held the door open for each other, smiled, and said hello. That didn't happen at home. I often thought, *I don't have time for this, I'm in a hurry here.* But they were being kind, and we need more of that in our world, don't we? I just didn't appreciate it then.

Reflection:

I went to Dallas kicking and screaming. I knew Texas would be a daunting change; it was a whole new and different world. I was scared and nervous. Not only would I be living in what I perceived as a foreign land, I was starting my surgery residency in a program with a widespread reputation for being "malignant."

This reputation in medical circles arose because it was well-known that the residents were worked unmercifully. At least one or two residents would be fired every year, which was unheard of in other surgery programs. What actually happened was that I met new people I would have otherwise never met; I developed lifelong friendships; I discovered my love for steak and Mexican food. And I learned how to become a surgeon.

Turned out that the UTSW program was not malignant. Our mentors, teachers, and attending surgeons wanted us to be the best of the best, so a lot was expected from us. Their strict supervision and constant prodding was all done with the best intentions, and for that I could not fault them. How could I? It made us all better surgeons. Turned out that moving to Texas was one of the best things that has ever happened to me.

With my surgery residency came maturity and growth as a person. I became more confident in who I was, in what I did, in my personal and professional relationships, and in what I had to offer the world. Sometimes, the only way to do that is to feel lost first.

The Yerkes–Dodson law developed by Robert M. Yerkes and John Dillingham in 1908 states that performance increases as stress increases, and performance decreases as stress decreases. This is what the concept of comfort zones is rooted in. If you push yourself just past the comfort zone, you can reach the growth zone. This comes with some anxiety and uncertainty, but this is where you do just that. You grow. With growth comes an increase in self-confidence and resilience. You don't have to take huge jumps and leaps; sometimes those can even have a negative effect with debilitating stress. But take those small steps, reach those small goals you set for yourself, and eventually this will lead to beautiful results.

My maternal grandmother.

Dad's parents.

Movie theater.

A photo of my parents on their wedding day.

Dad with the kids. L to R: Me, Dad, my brother.

Me in India.

My maternal grandfather with my mom on a family trip to Washington, DC.

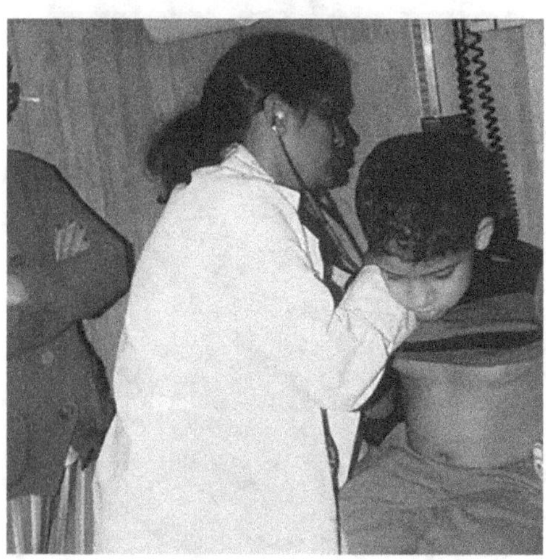

Mom in her clinic.

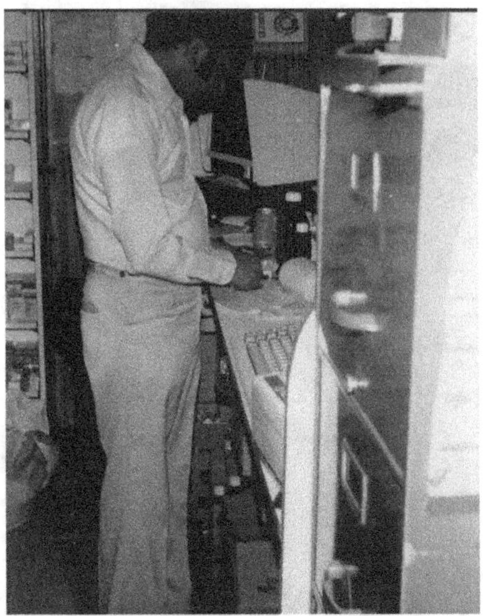

Dad in pharmacy.

Medical school graduation. L to R: Dad, brother, me, Mom.

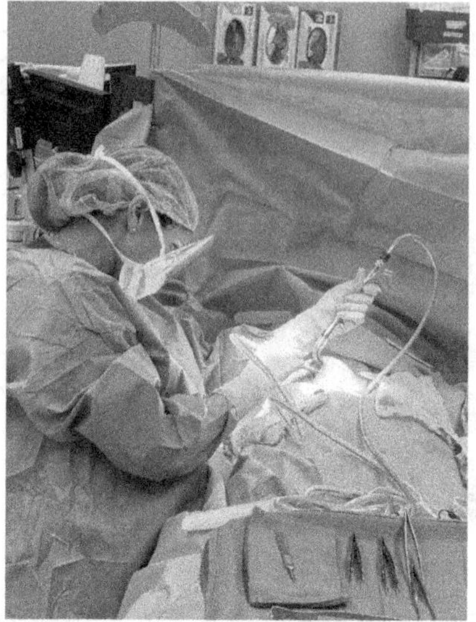

Me operating on a patient.

Me speaking on the Tamron Hall Show.

A photo of me and my husband, Andrew, on our wedding day.

Chapter Six

New Resident—of Texas

Parkland Hospital in Dallas is legendary. It was to this large county hospital that the gravely wounded President John F. Kennedy was taken after he was shot and where he was pronounced dead. (Lee Harvey Oswald was brought here two days later.) Parkland was and is run like a well-oiled machine, quite the opposite of many other county hospitals across the country.

At the time I arrived, every single department was uniformly excellent, from OB/GYN to Internal Medicine, staffed with well-trained dedicated residents and doctors. Parkland was a tertiary care hospital, meaning it had the capabilities to offer the highest level of care with access to every medical and surgical specialty. This included everything from Level 1 trauma, high-risk pregnancies, and every surgical specialty under the sun. Parkland was also a designated burn center serving northern Texas, Arkansas, and Oklahoma so we saw some of the worst burn cases in the region.

I felt privileged to work there; our patients were amazing. They were all so grateful for our care. Many of them had never received regular medical care and would show up in the ER with eroding breast cancer, for example, or cancer on their scalp where you could see bone when first examining them. Some even had gangrene of their feet to the point that there were maggots (yes, maggots) in their wounds—which, shockingly, is a good sign because they were essentially debriding the wound for us and preventing the infection from spreading and causing sepsis. Many of these men and women didn't have insurance and couldn't afford medical care. They were some of the kindest and most grateful patients I have ever had the privilege of caring for.

First year of residency—intern year—was a shock. The following story is really the best way to sum up this first year. Residency runs on a July 1-to-June 30 calendar year, so July 1 is everyone's first day. Mine happened to be on a busy Saturday, and I was on call covering emergency general surgery and a few other specialties, including colorectal surgery. On this particular day, my third-year resident had evaluated a sick patient who was having issues and called me to come up to his room to assist. In the meantime, he got a STAT page from the trauma hall and ran off but told this patient's nurse to keep an eye out for me. She asked who I was and what I looked like; his response was, "Look for the girl that looks like a deer in headlights."

This was a perfect description for all of us. We went from eight years of higher-level, mostly classroom, learning to the real deal, caring for actual, living, patients that could die. We all had MDs after our names, but not one of us felt like we had the knowledge and hands-on experience to deserve those letters. Not then, not yet. Everything was thrown at us at once. We either sank or swam but many of us just treaded water barely staying afloat, especially in those first few months.

It was a crazy year. We often felt alone on our little island trying to survive, but ultimately the one overriding task of our group was to learn how to care for patients on the floor. Our job was to manage them while they were in the hospital, from admission through surgery and post-operative care to discharge. This was the year when we had to learn how to identify if a patient was sick and when to "bump it up"—meaning to notify our direct superiors. We were the senior residents' eyes on the ground, so that they could have a pulse on all the patients in their care while they were operating. More important, while we had some flexibility in the care we provided, we were ultimately the collectors of information for the rest of the team and the executors of the plan of care.

When things were slow on the floor and we had some downtime, we were able to go to the operating room and watch what the rest of the team was doing. If we were lucky, we even got to scrub in and assist or close an incision. The middle of the night while we were on call was always the perfect time to get some experience in the OR with amputations or incision and drainage procedures. As interns we were certainly the low men (and women) on the totem pole, but this was the year in which our foundation was built.

Intern year is also the year you have to prove yourself. You are the new person, so everything you do is watched under a magnifying glass by everyone that matters. Any mishap can make the rest of your residency more difficult than it already is. You will be treated worse, scrutinized, and, even worse than that, any other mistakes, going forward, will always be unforgivable. But, if you work hard, listen, study, make your senior residents look good, and show up early and leave late, you get some slack when you make a mistake. I made every effort to start off on the right foot. I was a good rule follower and did well under pressure, so I thrived. Eventually, intern year became smooth sailing.

During this first year I was missing everything about the Northeast. It was such a culture shock; I still could not accept that I was living in Texas. In fact, knowing that I could transfer during my second year and head back to the Northeast was always a comforting thought. I was so adamant that I would not become a "Texan" that I even boycotted Mexican food. I'm not sure why this gave me some reassurance, but I literally did not eat Tex-Mex for a whole six months! (Mexican food is now one of my favorites; what was I thinking?)

But gradually, over time, I came to realize that Parkland was a great institution and the best possible place to train. This was due to the incredible surgeons I observed and learned from. They were the best of the best in their fields. They were invested in our education even though, more often than not, they were very hard on us. Regardless, all were generous with their knowledge. Many of these men—and they were mostly men, for sure—were older, getting ready to retire. I was quite aware that they were an invaluable repository of accumulated knowledge and wisdom gained over long distinguished surgical careers. I was lucky enough to receive the benefit of all their wisdom.

I realized it would be crazy to leave Parkland. As intern year came to a close, I talked a lot with friends in other programs. What they told me about their own experiences confirmed what exceptional training as a surgeon I was really receiving. I would only be doing myself a disservice by leaving, for New York, or any other program.

So, I made it through intern year. And Dallas had grown on me. I became friends with my fellow interns—some of whom formed an especially tight group over the next few years. I began dating a resident one year ahead of me in the program. I was fully immersed and committed to the program. I was coming to love all kinds of things about life in Texas. The world-class steak and Tex-Mex food. The "dive" bars where all the young women wore their best clothes and highest stiletto heels—or cowboy boots. Yes, I even started to like country music—although, if I'm being honest, this didn't happen until years later, right as I was getting ready to leave Texas. I found a new apartment in Uptown that I liked better. All the cool trendy shops, bars, and restaurants were in walking distance. Life as a transplant from the Northeast was looking much brighter.

***

Residency was all-consuming, taking over every waking hour of our lives. We worked thirty-hour shifts every third night. The hospital *was* our life. Our co-residents were our family. Taking care of patients who were critically ill and in need of life-saving operations was an awesome responsibility. When not at the hospital we were studying and prepping for cases the next day or the infamous Chief's conference every Wednesday.

In the weekly conference a resident would present a patient case (it might be any case falling under the large umbrella of general surgery) in a large auditorium. Then our program director would randomly call on residents to answer questions ranging from anatomy to surgical steps to disease processes. The director started with interns and worked his way up to the fifth-year residents. The more unprepared we were, the harder he was on us. Being put on the spot, it was not a pretty sight, and did not get easier as the years went by.

Chief's conference was followed by trauma conference every Friday. It too worked very much on the Socratic method but was held in a much smaller conference room. Again, a resident would present a trauma patient's case from time of their arrival to the trauma bay, in the emergency room and go through each step of their care. This would include any studies or tests performed, the surgery they may have required, and any post-surgery complications. The difference in this conference was that here the presenter would often be berated for any misstep or delay in patient care, and questions would then be directed to any resident in the audience.

At work I, along with my co-residents, was constantly on high alert, knowing that people were evaluating us at every single point along the way. A resident or two got fired every year; the program was strict. Parkland had high (very high!) expectations. *I could lose my job at any second; then what do I have? I am only educated and trained to do this one thing. I'm not qualified for any other job than this*—was my panicky thought on some of my toughest nights.

The surgery path is not for everybody: a calling where you have to be "on" all the time, not make mistakes, and crucially, work well with others. Some of my classmates who had made it all the way through tough medical schools and landed their dream residency had a rude awakening once they became surgical residents. These people realized early on: *I don't think surgery is for me.* So they changed direction, or left medicine altogether.

I knew surgery was for me. The patient lives I was dealing with were always paramount in my mind and those of my classmates. We were all in it together. We had put everything we had into being here. At this point, we had already spent eight years working toward landing this residency spot. Call it determination or just fear of losing it all, but we were going to get through and be the best surgeons we could be.

Reflection:

I've often thought about what motivated me to keep going through the toughest days (and nights) of residency. I wish I could truly say it's because I loved my job, but that would be a lie. I truly think it was my inability to give up on something or to accept failing at something. I had never failed, nor had I ever given up on anything. Quitting because things got hard was not an option. I had seen it with my parents, who worked endlessly and gave their careers and businesses 1,000 percent. They faced struggles of every kind, including health mishaps, but they pushed through and built something meaningful. I watched them as a child and absorbed their work ethic. The more challenging things were, the harder they worked. They pushed through.

Although, I'd be silly to say I could do what they did. Move to a new country and build a life and career from scratch without family support or finances. I had picked up so much from them without even realizing. But with hard work comes big rewards. I ultimately knew this. Work hard now, sacrifice now, enjoy life later. Or in my case, still work hard and sacrifice but still enjoy life. That "work hard, play hard" theme holds true to this day.

Sometimes, when I found time to sneak away for a minute or two to catch up with one of my co-residents, several said, "I can't picture you as a general surgeon." This was always really surprising to me. "What are you talking about? I *am* a general surgeon." I had never said or expressed a desire for anything else.

"I don't know—" these people always found it a bit hard to put their impression of me into words. "I just see you as someone who would want to make people look good. You just have that look of a plastic surgeon."

It happened often enough that I began to revisit my plastic surgery sub-internship days as a medical student. I really had loved it, but I would never admit that to anyone. Word spreads fast in residency, and that desire could really ruin things for me if my attendings and program director caught wind. Yet I would be lying if I wasn't secretly proud that I was giving off "plastic surgery vibes."

My dad had noticed how excited I was during my plastic surgery stint in medical school. He was fully on board with my quest to complete my general surgery residency. But he used to tell all the people at his manufacturing plant, starting in my earliest intern days, "Oh, my daughter will become a plastic surgeon someday." He was quite sure. The first time I caught wind of this on a quick visit home I was surprised. "Dad, what are you talking about? I like plastic surgery, but I haven't decided on anything yet!" Dad just smiled. He knew something I didn't.

***

In our second year of residency, we advanced to the next level: critical care. We were now managing the surgical ICU (intensive care unit), in charge of the burn unit, and saw all the surgery consults. For any patient who needed a surgeon, as second-year residents we were the first ones called. I would see the patients and present their cases, assessments, and plans to my third-year resident or even a chief resident, depending on the rotation. If we were on call, you could bet money that your pager would never stop going off. You'd have a list of patients that needed to be seen by you, so you'd have to do triage. See the sickest first, the ones that likely needed surgery. The others would have to wait.

In between running around the entire hospital seeing every patient that needed a surgery consult (or often, any patient with an unclear diagnosis) we were able to do a bit more actual operating. We began with the bread-and-butter kind of surgeries: hernia repairs, gall bladder surgeries, amputations. The hands-on experience was great, and the second year of general surgery was most challenging. This was the year when we were on call *all the time.* Every third day. If intern year didn't break you, this one would—at least in our program. Every year seemed worse than the previous, with more at risk than the year prior to that.

A big part of what made second year so terrible was our initial sense of confidence. After all, we made it through intern year—not much could phase us by June of that year. We had a false sense of security and confidence. Second year was a big slap in the face that humbled us very quickly. We had no direct supervision like we'd had during intern year, and we were responsible for the sickest patients in the burn ICU, the surgical ICU, and trauma hall. We quickly learned that we were nowhere near as prepared as we'd thought.

Though we had a lot of responsibility, we were still in the early years of learning. We were burn boss, meaning we were in charge of the Burn Center (where the Parkland formula for fluid replacement, that every hospital across the world uses when managing burn patients, was developed). We ran the trauma hall, meaning all Level 1 and Level 2 traumas were triaged and evaluated by us.

If we were lucky and the OR was "quiet," we would have senior backup for the Level 1's—the very worst traumas.

I vividly remember several times when I thought, *I'm just not cut out for this.* In July of my second year, I started in the surgical ICU (SICU). July 1 was a Sunday, and the resident from the night before had to leave before I came in so they could "round on" and evaluate patients on their new surgical service. There were no other residents there and while the surgical ICU fellow was present and had insight into the patients' care, he was operating and unavailable. Trauma was busy and everyone else that could be helpful was in the OR with the attending and the rest of the trauma team. This left me without a thorough run-through from the shift before or any plans for patients moving forward other than a sheet of paper with very basic patient information written out on it.

I was left alone with patients who were literally dying. Some were being sent straight from the trauma hall to make room for new traumas. These patients were unstable, bleeding, vitals crashing; just waiting for the OR. I relied on the nurses. I remember standing at the foot of one patient's bed in particular and thinking, *what am I doing?! I literally don't know what to do to help this person!*

Another Saturday night that second year I was down in trauma hall. The attending on call was notoriously known as being a black cloud. We were hit with trauma after trauma: stab wounds, gunshots, people literally arriving by the car loads due to being involved in car accidents. The hall was so busy, I had to put patients with stab wounds to the neck in the hallways in the ER and have my interns evaluate them, because there was someone else in worse shape I had to attend to. On nights like this, I could not wait for 7 a.m. and checkout time to come. Still,

I knew the shift would end with multiple attendings screaming at me for not personally looking at CT scans or not having lab or test results. We were so busy that there was no way that any of that would be possible, but that didn't matter. I'd just have to take all the abuse silently, which I did.

***

During this whole process, eyes were on us, evaluating every move. Could we handle the stress of second year? Were we on top of our game? Were our knowledge and skills improving? Could we be trusted with the sickest of the sick? While we welcomed the responsibility, we were not yet reaping the benefits, which for any surgery resident is being in the operating room, performing complex surgeries on very sick patients. Instead, we were getting patients ready for our senior residents to operate on. This, I think, was truly the breaking point for me and many of my co-residents. Though we did all the work, we didn't get to do what we were there for: operate.

We felt taken advantage of at times, on top of being constantly sleep-deprived and frustrated. At one point my morale sank so low that I was thinking about quitting altogether. I wasn't alone; things were so bad that our program director at the time took our whole class out for happy hour in the hopes of hearing us out and lifting our spirits. This sort of outing was unheard, of as this man was the one in charge of our futures at the program; he was scary. All of us tried to just fly under the radar with him in those early years. Happy hour was a nice effort, but all in all, things didn't get better because that year was a necessary evil.

It wasn't all unrelieved misery. One day, one of my attendings told one of the fellows on service, "You should try to convince

Smita to go into vascular surgery—she has good hands." These words came from Dr. Claggett, a world-renowned vascular surgeon and the originator of many innovative surgical procedures. The "good hands" comment was an unexpected boost for exhausted me, approaching thirty hours on my feet. His comment was literally life-changing; I felt so proud and supercharged. Good hands were a fortunate skill to possess. Surgical procedures can be taught and refined through study and practice. What every aspiring surgeon does not have are "good hands" something that is innate, or an artistic eye, which led to my continued interest in plastic surgery.

Second year nearly broke us, but I—and most of my classmates—made it through. Finally, mercifully, second year came to a close.

Reflection:

No matter how bad things get, time always moves forward. Each season passes. It always does. Those days as a second-year resident were some of the most trying times. But despite how bad things got, we knew deep down that we just needed to stick it out, time would pass, and these days would be behind us. We needed to learn, and sometimes we learned by just being thrown to the wolves. Sink or swim. We survived because there was no other option.

Being out of your comfort zone is when things can change for the better. Second year was necessary to learn how to evaluate sick surgical patients and prepare them for surgery. We learned how to care for the sickest burn, trauma, and ICU patients. We could not be great surgeons without building this foundation, even if we all wanted to skip right to the surgery part.

Nobody knows what it's like to be a resident except another resident. Nobody knows what it's like to be a surgery resident at UT Southwestern other than another surgery resident at UT Southwestern. No one else truly understands how tired you are, how overstretched, how at the mercy of emergencies you are. My boyfriend and I understood very well: if one of us got paged, there went our plans for the night. No problem, on either of our parts, as our plans typically involved studying at Starbucks for our cases the next day, sneaking in a quick workout, and grabbing some food. These were our dates. We were both in survival mode; we had no space to give more. The focus on both our sides was very much on our careers, as top efforts at work were required at all times.

This is not to say that other residents weren't pairing off, getting married, even having kids. I just had a different priority in this very limited time and space. What never even crossed my mind during that time was that these years of residency for women were also our most fertile years, our entire twenties and much of our thirties. I was far too exhausted to even consider any possible ramifications of that.

Things didn't get easier during third year. We had more responsibilities but also had more autonomy and ownership. Our newfound autonomy made this year much more palatable than previous years. In retrospect, this was likely my first sign that autonomy was something I needed in my career for fulfillment. The interns and second-year residents now reported to us. I was now in charge of the entire service—this included all the patients that were admitted while we were on call, all patients that we operated on or needed operations, even patients that were discharged in the past but had to come back due to complications.

Our program differed from other surgical programs in the country where the chief resident (fifth-year resident) was in charge. For us, it was third year when we "rounded" on patients with our junior residents, saw the consults, made a treatment plan, executed it, and "ran the list" with our chiefs to keep them in the loop. Rarely did they have any input or changes, unless you made a mistake, and rarely did they see the patients in person—again, only if you made a mistake. The more uninvolved your chief, the better. That meant you were doing well.

Most important, this was our big year to operate, to do those complex cases we longed to do. As a junior resident I had seen and scrubbed into every kind of surgery multiple times, but in each case, I watched the senior resident do the surgery with the third-year resident at the time. It was now my time to show up and do the surgeries.

Reflection:

My years of residency should have been my first clue that what really fulfills me is having autonomy, having a say. We had no autonomy our second year, but significantly less direct supervision than during intern year. Third year, while it was much harder with more responsibility, we had autonomy. I enjoyed that year because I learned a lot.

Fast forward to my first year of plastic surgery. I had just finished my general surgery residency. I was regarded as a junior attending. We were all operating and working independently. Plastic surgery was a culture shock. I was back at the bottom, having to report every minor occurrence and unable to make any decisions. Of course, this was necessary, as I was learning this new trade, but it was a tough year. This would come up again in my career after residency: the true reason behind my burnout and dissatisfaction in my first real job was my lack of autonomy. I had zero say in the type of patient or patient concern I saw. I had no control over the schedule both in my clinic and in my operating room. I had a vision of what I wanted my brand to be and the type of care I wanted to provide to my patients but I was significantly limited in this. I felt I had no voice.

There is clear evidence that autonomy fosters increased engagement and motivation. It creates ownership and a sense of pride in your work and contributions. While you might be working harder and possibly devoting more time and energy to your work, you are doing it on your terms and seeing your fruits of your labor.

Now I was in the OR for bigger surgeries with my fifth-year resident, who walked me through the complex cases and taught me along the way. The attending surgeon would sometimes scrub in according to the case, but at Parkland they usually did not. The program was very much about giving residents real, hands-on surgical experience. We lived by the "see one, do one, teach one" mantra.

I still did not narrow down which specialty I wanted to pursue. I really liked colorectal surgery; I really liked endocrine surgery. But as I was learning more about these areas on my specialized rotations, I had to start eliminating them from the constantly running checklist in the back of my mind. Ultimately, I knew I wasn't going to become a general surgeon. The field had changed, there were very few true general surgeons, and they were typically found in more rural settings. I was going to specialize in something. But the question was always: in what?

UT Southwestern had a reputation for being malignant. I absolutely did not agree with this reputation. We worked very hard, a lot was expected of us, but our attendings ultimately wanted us to succeed. They were not cruel and demanding just to be mean or enjoy seeing us fail. Having said that, we had super-high standards to uphold and not all of us succeeded. Every year or two a resident would get fired. This happened in the plastic surgery department as well, which would leave an open spot in that particular class.

It was not unheard of for someone in general surgery who was interested in plastic surgery, in the third year of residency, to fill the empty spot that had suddenly opened. Such an opening gave them the option to leave general surgery residency and continue their last two years in plastic surgery. I had seen it happen in classes above me, and sure enough, a spot opened in my third year of residency that was definitely of interest to me.

Plastic surgery remained a strong possibility on my ever-changing list of options. I knew another resident in my class who was absolutely committed to becoming a plastic surgeon. When that spot suddenly opened in our third year, he went for it. So, did I. He got the position, which was a huge blow to me, but I had to accept it was simply not meant to be. I had no way of knowing that what I took as a major setback would prove to be providential.

***

Another day of Grand Rounds Conference, a top surgeon from New York came to UT Southwestern as a visiting professor. This man, a renowned expert in pancreatic cancer, shared his knowledge about the latest cutting-edge treatments for this terrible disease, based on his extensive research and what he had learned over many years treating advanced cases. The pancreas has a head, a body, and a tail. He specifically stressed in his talk how a mass or tumor on the tail of the pancreas is a particularly dangerous sign with a grim prognosis. Discovered in that location, it was difficult to diagnose because these cases so often presented with few or no symptoms, when the disease was far too advanced for even surgery to make a difference.

I was dutifully paying close attention, taking notes, soaking up every word—but the minute I heard these words, the most random thought leaped into my mind. *If my father ever gets pancreatic cancer in the tail, I'll die.* I was now living far away, but I spoke with my father all the time. The moment there was any news in my life—good or bad, major or minor—my first act was to grab my phone and call my father. Big things, like when I failed to secure the plastic surgery residency spot. And every small thing. If I had a flat tire, he was the first call I made. He often would call AAA or a car shop from New Jersey for me. Dad was my touchstone.

There was simply no reason for such a dire scenario to pop unbidden into my head. It was unnerving, but I shook it off. Both my parents were fine. Dad was running his own successful generic pharmaceutical manufacturing business; Mom was retired from medicine and helping Dad as best as she could. My brother was attending school out of state and pursuing a pharmacy degree.

My parents had summoned him for the very same conversation they'd had with me four years before. He had originally been leaning toward orthopedics, but this time, my parents prevailed. They convinced him to switch to pharmacy with an eye to joining the family business. He was busy, happy in Baltimore, and deeply absorbed in his own studies. In short, everyone in my family was good. I plunged back into my work.

Reflection:

Looking back at the decision from a vantage point of many years later, I have to admit there is a part of me that will always regret not taking my parents' advice to not pursue medicine. In fact, as an adult I understand that in nearly everything my parents said, did, and advised, they were right. I think about how different my life would have been had I just gone to pharmacy school and learned the family business from my dad.

Don't get me wrong: I love plastic surgery. But now I realize how truly absurd the demands on my time and lifestyle were all those years. I sacrificed everything for my training. I gave up my twenties and half of my thirties to become the surgeon I am. I missed big events in my friends' lives, I lost touch with many, I lost so much valuable time that could have been spent with my family, especially my dad. I worked endless hours on little to no sleep. I was earning minimum wage for a forty-hour work week but, given how many hours I actually spent working, my pay was significantly less. This added up to years and years' worth of lost earnings. Not to mention, I was at my unhealthiest, physically and mentally, during these years.

My brother, too, would forge his own path and ultimately did not take over the family business. Dad would eventually sell it. My brother obtained two professional and doctorate degrees and was really making a name for himself at the Food and Drug Administration at a young age. He found his path; I found mine. Choosing a field in medicine is not a choice you make for the prestige or the money. It's truly because you have a calling. Maybe life as a pharmacist would have been satisfying and rewarding and taken significantly less out of me. Or, perhaps, I would have been unfulfilled, always regretting that I hadn't gone for that dream. Ultimately, though, I truly believe that there is a plan for us all and becoming a plastic surgeon was and is mine.

Fourth year of residency meant more rotations. I was now working on intricate and complicated cases, such as kidney and liver transplants and cardiac surgery, and I loved these surgeries. Still, I really needed to revisit the idea of plastic surgery as I was slowly crossing other specialties off my list as I gained more experience. Plastic surgery wasn't a scheduled rotation during fourth year, so I had to make special arrangements with my program director. My plastic surgery rotation was the most eye-opening month of my training to date. I had thought my general surgery program was intense. Plastic surgery was a whole different world. The intensity of the program was overwhelming—but I absolutely fell in love with the surgeries I was seeing. They were challenging in an entirely new way; the artistic element and problem-solving came into play, which was deeply satisfying and refreshing.

Being back in plastic surgery as a fourth-year surgery resident as opposed to a fourth-year medical student felt like a completely different experience. I had a far better grounding in surgery, medicine, patient needs, and so many other variables. I had a more mature eye, and finally knew that this was, without a doubt, what I needed to do. That month led to my deciding moment. The light went on. This was it. I had to pursue this path.

Except...

I had been working so hard, for five years. And I was well aware that plastic surgery was an extremely demanding and exacting field. UT Southwestern Plastic Surgery had an even worse reputation for being malignant than General Surgery. The goal was to produce the best plastic surgeons, but the methods were harsh. As much as I had loved my brief rotation, as much as I was now committed to becoming a plastic surgeon, I was not about to sign up for three more years of that level of intensity. I met with my program director to touch base after my rotation. He, in not so many words, told me that if I wanted a spot at UT Southwestern, he would make sure that happened. I, however, was not sold. I needed to explore other programs first. After a long, grueling five-year general surgery program, I honestly felt like I shouldn't have to and I certainly didn't want to, in my short-sighted view at the time, work harder than I had already worked. I also was ready to move on from Texas. I needed to see what else was out there. I can't say he wasn't surprised by this answer, but he accepted it and we moved on.

Once again, I did a round of interviews, traveled out of state—the whole process. And every time I compared what I was seeing to my very own home program, my choice became clearer.

A pivotal car ride with a close friend and co-resident sealed the deal. We carpooled to a welcome reception for the applicants the night before interviews. He was always the voice of reason and also very blunt. "Smits, this is the best program in the world, you'd be an idiot to miss this opportunity." Sold. There was no way I could leave and go to another program. I was already at the best place; he was right. The plastic surgery residency at Southwestern was the best—officially ranked No. 1. Demanding as it would be, why would I leave? I was never one to shy away from hard work—why start now?

Back I went to my program director. "I was wrong. This is the best program. I want to stay and do my plastic surgery residency here."

He had known I'd be back in his office once I realized how great a program it was. He also knew that I needed to explore these other programs so there was no question in my mind. Without a blink of an eye, he told me to set up a meeting with the chair of Plastic Surgery, a man even scarier than my program director sitting in front of me. Which I did. I was confident that this was where I needed to be—and, yes, was meant to be. I could not walk away from the best training program in the world. I wanted to be the best of the best, and this was the only place I could do that.

On this match, I ranked my very own school, UT Southwestern, as No. 1. I'd like to think it ranked me No. 1 as well, but regardless, I was staying in Texas for three more years when my residency finished and going for the best plastic surgery training in the nation. And I was thrilled.

Reflection:

I had gone through an entire year thinking that I had done my time, that I'd already put in the work. It was time to opt for an easier path and get to the next level. I was exhausted from the 200 percent effort put into pre-med, medical school, and now general surgery. Taking the easier path seemed like a great idea, except when I realized that once this opportunity passed, there was no turning back. Doors and opportunities might be closed. Why would I do that? Taking the easy way out now would only make things harder for me later.

A very important concept: Taking the easy way can lead to negative consequences down the road. You miss opportunities to develop life skills, such as resilience or how to approach problems. You aren't prepared for the challenges that life throws your way because you haven't developed these skills. Ultimately, you might find yourself in a position in life where you are unfulfilled. Whether it's work, your personal life, or your accomplishments. All of this defines who we are and who we become.

What I learned from this is to walk through every door that you are fortunate to have open for you—or that you forced open yourself. Do the work, put in the time, it will only make you better and stronger. It will give you bigger and better opportunities for your future.

Chapter Seven

When Love, Medicine, and Even Miracles Fail

With my future plastic surgery residency at Parkland all set, I continued my fifth and final year of my general surgery residency. I had finally moved my way up to being on the right side of the OR table. For the past four years I'd been on the left side of the table (the patient's left) because that's more of an assistant position. In fifth year, as a chief resident, I was on the right side of the table as the primary surgeon. This was the apex of all residents' increased responsibilities during this final year of learning and training.

On a Monday morning, Labor Day, I was preparing to scrub in for a big surgery where we would be operating on the pancreas—a Whipple procedure, used to treat pancreatic cancer when there is a mass in the head of the pancreas. I was talking with the chief of the department, the attending for the case, when I got multiple urgent cell phone calls from my mother. I thought that was odd; she never called in the morning as she knew I'd be in surgery. I picked up. Dad had a mass on *his* pancreas; they were going to do further testing. She was told it was cancer. I didn't want to believe her, so I had her put my dad on the phone. He told me the same story.

I was shocked, but my case was about to start. I had to call my boyfriend at the time, who was now a fellow at my program, to touch base with my mom and call the OR directly if there were any emergencies. I told the surgeon I was operating with that day, "My dad is in the ER, I might get a phone call that I'll have to answer." He understood, but no call came. I was all business throughout the long surgery, putting the terrible news out of my mind as I focused on the patient in front me. Compartmentalizing would soon become something I became very good at.

By the time I scrubbed out almost seven hours later, more of my dad's test results were back, and they were not promising. Pancreatic cancer in the tail of the pancreas that had metastasized to the abdomen, also known as drop metastasis. I headed over to the private university hospital across the street, a short drive from Parkland Hospital, where I had to meet with another attending surgeon to "round on" our ICU patients. He pulled me aside as soon as I arrived and said, "You need to go home." I was surprised; I hadn't told anybody except my boyfriend and the surgeon I had just left what was going on.

"What do you mean? I can't just leave."

"Nope. You need to go." My boyfriend had gotten ahold of him while I was operating to explain the situation. My attending was a surgical oncologist; he knew what that news meant. He reassured me that he'd talk to our chairman and I had nothing to worry about regarding my duties. I had to focus on my dad.

The great blessing of this situation was that many of the surgeons I had been working with had trained at Memorial Sloan

Kettering in New York City, the pre-eminent cancer hospital. In just a few hours my current surgical oncology attendings had already called their friends there, renowned experts in the field, and lined up immediate help for my dad. His first appointment was in a few days, with a world-class surgeon and medical oncologist who was booked months in advance.

Had I been in a plastic surgery residency at that point, I would not have had these relationships so well established. I was now in the position to be able to pick up the phone and ask for favors with no fear. The professional and personal bonds built over the past four years allowed me the precious time off to be with my father for all his preliminary appointments. First, with the surgical oncologist and then the various other doctors who would be handling chemotherapy and everything else.

During the most stressful week of my life to date, I could only be grateful that I had not gotten that plastic surgery opening. How devastated I had been when I did not win that prized spot in plastic surgery as a third-year resident. But now I was able to be present for my father. And that was the only place I wanted to be.

Reflection:

There's a saying, "If you get what you want, it's God's direction, if you don't, it's God's protection." This could not hold truer than in this instance. I had been upset, disappointed, and angry that I hadn't gotten that open plastic surgery spot when, in so many ways, I had been the better and more qualified resident. It didn't make sense until now. God was protecting me, knowing what would happen over the next few years.

As a surgical resident it was so terribly hard to wrap my head around this development. To hear a diagnosis like the one my dad received was to know the end of this particular story. Surgeons know a death sentence when they hear one. With a tumor in the worst possible location, at the tail of the pancreas and already metastasized, the patient doesn't recover, doesn't go into remission, can't be operated on; his life span can only be measured in months. I steadied myself for the ordeal ahead, knowing I had every possible resource at my disposal. So much good will, experience, and knowledge available to help my father. We would all pull together.

***

As a chief resident, my schedule was finally a bit more consistent. I now had every other weekend off, so I was able to fly home twice a month to be at my father's side; my brother and I traded off weekends. I could call on co-residents if I happened to be on home call for a Saturday, who would cover for me so I could be in New Jersey. And I was really needed there; my mother was not doing well. All her training and medical knowledge seemed to fly out the window during this time. Every development was brand new to her. With any setback or piece of bad news, she would fall apart. She was a wife, not a doctor, during this ordeal, unable to even give me coherent updates over the phone when I called from Dallas to check in. It was literally like talking to someone with zero medical background. It was very stressful.

Over the months, my dad rallied quite well to the invasive treatments, including chemotherapy. He had a truly remarkable response. During this trying time, some family friends in India called my parents about their son, who was in the States going to college. The school that he was attending suddenly closed, and he was abruptly on his own. He now had no place to live, no school to attend, and no family in the States. There were numerous phone calls back and forth from India; in times like this it is not uncommon for young Indians in the United States to stay at an auntie and uncle's house in the community. My parents agreed that this young man could stay at their house until he sorted out his future. Another blessing in disguise.

My priority was spending time with my father. I told him on one of those alternate weekends at his side, "I don't have to finish general surgery to start plastic surgery. I might quit, that way I can be at home and spend time with you. I can still start plastic surgery as planned."

You can imagine my dad's response. Without skipping a beat: an immediate and firm "no." There was no way that he was going to let me not finish what I started, especially after witnessing all the years of hard work and sacrifice. My father's entire life had been about putting in the work to allow us to get the best possible education and supporting us in succeeding in our chosen fields. I could not go against his wishes now, and ultimately, I knew he was right. So I flew back and forth between Dallas and New Jersey every other weekend while keeping up my role as fifth-year chief.

My family certainly knew what we were facing. As a general surgeon—in a surgical oncology rotation at the time—I was treating many patients suffering from pancreatic cancer. I regularly did resections and removed tumors. However, the patients in my dad's situation, we never even saw. They were too progressed, not surgical candidates; we only saw the patients who had cancer that could still be operated on. My dad was not in that position; his cancer was metastatic; it had spread. Still, the punishing chemo was, amazingly, a success.

Five months into his treatment, my father had a follow-up CT scan to check his progress. He was in the hospital at this point, having been admitted for dehydration. Incredibly, all of the metastatic cancer appeared to have vanished, and his tumor had shrunk to a fraction of its original size. His blood work was great: the tumor markers were close to zero.

This sort of result simply does not happen with that type of cancer. I had already accepted that I couldn't doctor my way out of this situation, so my surgeon mentality had vanished; my faith kicked in. Surely if a miracle could occur, it would happen for my father. All the signs were so positive; I truly believed my dad would be the one person to beat the statistic of three to five months' life expectancy.

It was my brother's weekend, so I was working away in Dallas. For some reason that entire week, I wasn't able to get my dad on the phone. It was odd, between calling the nurses, calling his room, his cell phone, having my mom try to call when she was there, we just could not connect. So, I had asked my boyfriend, who was in town visiting my family, to help. "When you get to my dad's room, can you please call me? I have not been able to reach him all week."

I finally got that call. He was having a great deal of difficulty hearing, most likely a side effect of his medications. As I was trying to talk to him, the connection kept breaking up; we couldn't hear each other. At the end of our call I said, "OK, Dad, I love you!"

"I love you," he said. The only words on that entire call I heard clearly. And we hung up. The hospital had made plans to finally discharge him on Monday; my mom arranged for a hospital bed to be delivered to their home. Everything was set; my brother was there. We were living our very own miracle.

***

My brother and father's relationship had been a bit stressed and strained in the past few years. I generally followed my parents' wishes, while, typical of many younger siblings, my brother had a much more defiant personality overall. My brother was with Dad on the Saturday night after we got the good news that he'd soon be coming home. My boyfriend had also showed up to visit with him, and Mom was coming in and out. Dad hadn't shaved in forever, so my brother shaved him. He looked much better, which lifted his spirits. Dad asked that Chinese food from his favorite place be brought in—he really did love his spareribs. The three of them ate Chinese food in his room that night, it was all very convivial.

In the middle of the night, Dad woke up and asked my brother for a cup of coffee.

"Dad, it's two o'clock in the morning, why would you want to drink coffee right now?"

"Can you just get it for me."

My brother dutifully went down the hallway, got coffee from the empty breakroom, and sat and drank coffee with my dad and talked. Then a fatherly reminder: "Mom's and Smita's birthdays are coming up, be sure to get them roses," he said to my brother. My dad got us flowers—roses—every year, every birthday, no matter where I was, even if I was on-call at the hospital. He always found a way to get flowers to me on my birthday.

My brother agreed. They finished their chat, and I'm sure whatever they spoke about gave my dad some peace that we would be okay. And then Dad went to sleep and didn't wake up the next day.

I got a phone call early the next morning, a Sunday morning. He wasn't waking up, his organs shut down, he didn't have reflexes, though he was still breathing. I panicked and was in disbelief—he'd been hanging out chatting the night before without any issues. Everything had been looking so good! The rest of that morning was a blur. I somehow made it to the airport, got on a plane, and made it back to New Jersey.

A family friend came to pick me up at the airport and took me directly to the ICU. I called (or texted—again, a blur) one of my best friends from college who lived in New Jersey on the way. I think I said something like, "I'm back in NJ and heading to hospital…it doesn't look good." I walked into the ICU and saw my brother crying. I was shocked; I truly couldn't understand why the tears now. We'd gotten through so much, we'd pull through this crisis, too. I hadn't seen him cry since we were kids. I tried to walk past him to enter my dad's room, but he stepped in my way and pulled me in for a hug.

"Go see Mom," he said as he quickly collected himself.

I was confused. Why would I need to see Mom? But things were not clicking for me. I walked into the small family waiting room, where Mom was hysterical. She had been very up and down and emotional since my dad's diagnosis, so I still wasn't unduly alarmed. There were family friends there consoling her. Still thinking this was all very weird, I headed into my dad's room. It was quiet, my dad looked like he was asleep.

After a few seconds, I noticed there were no sounds in the room. The machines were all turned off. I approached my dad and touched him. He was cold. He had passed—only days after receiving the most glowing progress report. My dad, my world, was no longer here. I was shocked. I simply couldn't process this development. I have no idea what happened afterward other than, as I was standing there, my friend whom I'd called from the car walked into the room, took in the situation immediately, and enveloped me in a hug. It was real. I fell apart.

It is my belief that we all have a time to go, in accordance with God's plan for each of us. This had been Dad's time, and I think he knew that and had accepted it. In fact, when I had met with the surgical oncologist and chairman of Surgery at the hospital, who had delivered the diagnosis to my dad, he said one thing that I'll never forget. "I've never seen this in my entire career, but when I told your dad about the positive biopsy results and the prognosis, he just said "If this is God's will, then let it be." He was calm and unphased. "That's my dad," I said. Unyielding in his faith and God's plan for him. The last month was more to prepare my mom, brother and me for life without him, unthinkable as that was.

It was a blessing that he passed in the hospital and not at home; I don't think my mom could have survived that. It was another blessing for my brother to have had that healing conversation on my dad's last night. Perhaps that was the one thing that Dad needed to settle before leaving this world. I think after his favorite dinner, and that discussion, he felt he could go.

Our last words "I love you" were my blessing. Still, it was important for me to get to the bottom of what I couldn't medically work out or understand. His body literally just stopped. There was no infection, no heart attack, his labs were all normal, even that morning. There was no sepsis, no infection, no heart attack or stroke. His organs just stopped. I simply couldn't make sense of it.

My boyfriend, a board-certified general surgeon and fellow in vascular surgery at the time, also looked at every single test and study done that weekend and that morning—all normal. There was no way to make sense of him passing other than that this was truly God's plan. The only way the rest of us could try to accept and understand it was with faith. This is life, and this is medicine. There is only so much we can do—as doctors and family members. I could only be thankful for every moment I'd had with him. He was a blessing in our lives, perfect in every sense of the word and we were lucky to have him, even though his time with us was cut extremely short.

***

I was Daddy's girl, had been all my life. As a child, I'd had literal nightmares that something might happen to him. Now, the very worst had happened, and it was every bit as devastating as I had feared. My mom was hit doubly hard; apart from losing her husband, she was now faced with practical matters like handling the finances and bills, as all this had been Dad's domain. My brother and I were both living out of state. Our mother was going to be forced to take on so many new responsibilities entirely on her own.

The big upside to the tight-knit Indian community was the enormous outpouring of support from all around her. Everyone rallied to her side. As helpful as her friends were at the beginning, though, they naturally had to return to their own lives and eventually started to come around less. The student family friend turned out to be a real gift; he wound up staying put for a good while, living there in the house with my mom. Another piece that seemed to have been perfectly placed. This gave us some peace of mind as my brother returned to his studies in Maryland and I flew back to finish my final year of residency in Dallas.

Once again, I knew my path forward.

Reflection:

My life was torn apart the day my dad passed away; there was life before, and then the new unthinkable reality of life without my father. Everything changed. I truly do not know how I survived this loss. I wish I could say as a doctor that I went through all the "official" phases of grief. I wish I could say as a Christian that I held firm in my belief in God's goodness. Neither would be true. While I believed that my father's passing was God's plan, that didn't mean that I didn't reject the plan. I immediately compartmentalized and dived back into work, studies and my many daily duties. I kept all my sorrow and anger completely separate from my life in Dallas, where I was extremely busy.

When I wasn't in the hospital or studying, I was running. I had hated outdoor running my entire life. I could run on a treadmill with music and a movie playing, but outdoors, I would stop and walk the second I got tired or bored. But that year, running became my escape. Mostly because I could clear my head and get into a zone, just listening to the beat of the music with my footsteps. That year I ran my first half-marathon. Since then, I've run countless half-marathons and five full marathons. Running became a part of my identity in 2011.

As far as my relationship with God: I was angry. I felt fooled by Him. How could my dad's scans and blood work look so good, and yet he was still taken from us? My dad was supposed to be the miracle, the one who would beat the statistics. But I soon realized that the true miracle was that my dad was now with God. He's pain free, stress free, in the most beautiful place, with our Creator. We, the ones left behind, are the ones that are left feeling pain and sadness.

They say time heals everything. It doesn't. There will always be a big hole in my heart and life without my dad around. Time just moves forward, and so do we, in a world that will never be the same.

Chapter Eight

A Brutal Training Ground: Becoming the Best

My life would never be the same and I knew it. Yet I had to keep going. I took two weeks off to arrange for my father's funeral and ensure that my mom would be OK. Then I dived back into work. It was hard and painful to leave Mom alone, but I had to finish residency. My dad had made it very clear that I was not to compromise my future to sit at home. So I shoved all my grief and sorrow to the back of my mind and returned to work.

Everyone I worked with offered sincere condolences, which I appreciated. However, every time someone did so, it made it impossible to keep my pain in a box and I would immediately feel the tears coming and have to hide away in the closest bathroom to collect myself. It's not that I wasn't appreciative—I could not have been more grateful for my colleagues' personal and professional support during his illness—but my dad was gone, and nothing was going to bring him back. Reminders at work were the last thing I needed.

Compartmentalizing was not the healthiest way to cope, but it was my way of getting through the worst loss of my life. My grief was a long and hard road. For months after my dad's death, when something would happen, or I'd have news to share, I would automatically grab my phone and start to call him before realizing.

I needed to focus. Plastic surgery is an extremely competitive field, and UT Southwestern, where I was finishing up my five-year general residency, had the No. 1 plastic surgery program in the entire country. All the plastic surgeons there knew me and were following my progress carefully. I now knew without a doubt that, had I gone to any of the five places I had ranked above UT Southwestern for my general surgery residency, there was zero chance I would have ended up in this prestigious plastic surgery program. Dallas really was the right place for me, and where I would remain for the next three years.

***

As a student in the midst of the grind that is medical school, it seems like the hardest undertaking ever. When you become a resident, you can only look back on medical school and realize how easy that really was compared to the process of becoming an actual surgeon. Plastic surgery residency was all those pressures combined—times 1,000.

I'd just come off five years of general surgery residency, with the final year spent as chief with a great deal of responsibility, authority, and autonomy. If a surgery patient started to code, we would immediately start CPR and take whatever measures were required. I wouldn't even call my attending until the crisis was over. Only then would I give him or her a heads up—this patient coded, but we brought him back, he has stabilized, all is well. That was all that needed to happen. "Great," the attending would say, and that was the end of that.

All of a sudden, I went from being at the top of the totem pole to the bottom rung. I now had to call my attendings for the most basic things, such as, "Can I remove this drain?" Being scolded for removing a drain that in their opinion should have been in longer. Critiquing my suturing—for which I had been lauded over the years. Suddenly, my sutures were being cut out, and I was told to start over. We had all just finished a demanding surgical residency, coming from a mindset of, *I'm a general surgeon! I'm saving lives!* Whatever we had done before didn't stop our new attendings from breaking down our egos. They put us in our place. Fast.

After a few months of this, I was quite sure I had made a big mistake. My second year of general surgery had been the most challenging of my life to date but compared to what I was facing every day here, it had been a cakewalk. I had known going into it that the program was tough, but I'd truly had no idea what was coming. This was a complete relearning experience. In plastic surgery, the anatomy is different, the parts of the body we were operating on were different, the expectations were certainly different. It got to the point where I felt, "If my plastic surgery attendings pushed the wrong button on the wrong day, I am out. I'm a board-certified general surgeon and I'll just leave and practice general surgery."

A good friend of mine, who had done five years of otolaryngology (ENT) at UT Southwestern and then gone on to a plastic surgery residency, was one year ahead of me. "You just have to get through the first six months," he told me, "Then they all back off." OK, I could do anything for six months.

His words were the only life preserver I had, and I held on tight. I had never worked so hard in my life, walking on the edge of fear and exhaustion, but I chugged along holding on to this idea that things were going to change in six months. Six months came and went and nothing changed. I went straight to this friend and called him out. "Things have not gotten better; they are still terrible!" His answer: "I had to tell you something—or you would have quit long ago!" I wasn't too happy with him at the time, but we still joke about that to this day.

I had to learn "the plastic surgery way." The difference between plastic surgeons and other surgeons is that it's all about what you see. For most surgeons, the priority is what's on the inside. The bone, the ligament, the tumor. Colon repairs, small bowel resections—it's all about what's going on inside the body. At the end of the operation, skin closure is almost an afterthought. For plastic surgeons, the skin cutting, draping, and each stitch *is* the result.

Every move made during plastic surgery needs to be done with consideration of how it will look one year from that day. We had to compensate for how skin settles and heals over time. Everything was different, including the intricacy of the procedures, the extremely detailed anatomy, the technical skills needed to suture blood vessels that were 1.5 mm in diameter together, and moving muscles from one part of the body to the other to reconstruct a soft tissue defect.

The cosmetic patient is a whole other beast. These patients are completely healthy, and we are introducing risks for them to help them to feel their best and most confident. The art that I found so appealing was also so frustrating as I was learning. There was never one correct solution to a patient's concern or problem as there had been in general surgery. If there was an intestinal injury, the way we would repair it was always consistent, down to the type of suture and how we sutured. In plastic surgery, there were many ways to skin a cat. If a patient wants a breast lift, for example, all surgeons have their own technique, their own way of orienting the scars or breast tissue. They use different sutures and different ways of suturing. There is no straightforward, single, correct answer. That is the "art" part of plastic surgery. While the fundamental principles are the same, the approach and execution vary greatly from surgeon to surgeon, making it challenging to learn.

My attendings were hard on me—they were extremely hard on all of us—but there was a method to their madness. They wanted to produce the best plastic surgeons in the country. For the entire first year of my plastic surgery residency, I avoided the bosses like the plague. This included our chairman and program director; I made every effort to stay out of their way. I had no desire to be under their scrutiny any more than I already was. At the time I did not fully appreciate that they were pushing me to become a better plastic surgeon and get out of my own way and my comfort zone. They saw my potential.

I was the only woman in my class, and the class above and below me, so it just happened that my colleagues were all guys. And they truly were like brothers to me. We all saw each other under the most intense stress, on the worst days of our lives. I can only liken it to something like being in the military; the bonds we built were strong. We were all going through the most intensive program imaginable. We had to have each other's backs and help each other. It was always them (our attendings) versus us. I was lucky that we had a tight group.

***

My dad had already told many people I was going to be a plastic surgeon; that knowledge kept me going. Still, there were more days than not, especially in that first year, that I wanted to quit. I reminded myself that I'm not a quitter. I don't fail. That's not how I was raised. So, I endured. Toward the end of my first year, my efforts began to pay off. My attendings could see that I put in the work and time. I showed up as ready as I could be, having read about the cases and done all possible preparation.

In fact, I completely shifted my sleep schedule to make sure I was most awake when studying and prepping. That meant dinner chased down with a Monster energy drink once I was home for the day sometimes around 7 p.m. or 8 p.m. I'd fall asleep (I was immune to Monster drinks by now). Wake up after my quick nap. Study until 11 p.m. and sleep until 2 a.m. I'd then study for the next two hours or so and make my way back to the hospital for rounds. I also reverted to my intern and medical school habits: be the first person to show up and the last to leave. Just be there all the time. And they noticed.

On the first day of my second year of my plastic surgery residency, which started in July, things were immediately different. The pressure eased, and I was thankful. We residents now had a far better understanding of the material. I had established a good reputation, which helped enormously. My attendings trusted me to show up and take the best possible care of patients—they had seen me do it for a year—so the monitoring went way down, a big relief.

We were now at the stage of refining and fine-tuning our technical skills on every sort of plastic surgery procedure. What was also a contributing factor in how drastically different second year was compared to first year was the confidence I had gained. I understood the material and medical studies better. I understood the procedures better.

By the third year we were allowed to focus more on our own interests, and we took on more of a junior attending role. The younger residents would ask for our help on complex operations; a role I truly enjoyed. By this final year of residency, plastic surgery had become fun and enjoyable. We had autonomy, we were respected; we also took on more of a mentor and educator role for our juniors; I felt like I was really making a difference.

I served as administrative chief resident my final year—the person to liaise between all the residents and the faculty. I did the call schedules, met every month with our program director, handled issues with the residents; if they had any sort of problem, I was the first person they came to. I was busy but thriving as the end of my three-year residency came into sight.

I was nothing if not a diligent and hard worker, as I had been for my entire life. I never got in significant trouble. I was never written up. That's not to say I didn't get into it with various nurses or residents along the way, but the thing about residency is if you have a good reputation, you can get away with a lot more than if you don't. So, it had been smooth sailing, at least in that regard, for eight straight years (and I use the term "smooth" loosely, as nothing in residency was smooth, but it could have been much worse). Then, in my very last month, I was doing a standard facelift. This was a resident case, where I was in charge.

In my OR that day was a nurse who had never assisted in plastic surgery and didn't know how to set up the room. I did my best to help her. This was an afternoon case, and we were already delayed, so all I wanted was to get things started and move along. I didn't know where the instruments were either, so I told her I'd step into the other OR where our usual plastic surgery tech was scrubbed in, to ask him where things were. She welcomed the help.

"I was actually about to scrub out and take my break, I'll just grab everything for you," he offered.

"Great!" I said. He accompanied me back into the OR, helped get us started, and the surgery proceeded smoothly from that point on. The case went fine; the patient did well. Then I found out I had been written up. By the original nurse on the case. When a resident gets written up, she must meet with the program director. I was called in for a meeting with him. I had no idea what was going on.

"The nurse claims you went over her head; that you *forced* another tech to come into the OR and help..."

I was completely confused, which I'm sure was written all over my face. I explained my recall of the day's events. How grateful I had been to get additional help to get the case started. That the OR nurse had also been grateful for the extra set of hands. How the surgery had proceeded smoothly from that point on.

"I believe you, but this kind of thing will come up again," my program director said. I truly had no idea what he was talking about; implying that while this may have been the first time I experienced an incident like this, it certainly would not be the last. Less than a year later, I would figure out exactly what he meant that day.

Reflection:

The real issue with this write-up was not about the events of the day or what happened in surgery. The real issue was that that I was a woman. The older female nurse—whom I had never worked with before or ever seen—no doubt felt intimidated that I came in confidently and acted like I was in charge. Which for all intents and purposes I was—it was a resident case; it was my case. The attending on record didn't walk in until we were well underway. I had people leave other rooms to help me, help us. While this was not my request, I had become friends with the OR staff, and that particular surgical tech specifically, over the years, so he wanted to help.

I was younger, female, and assertive. I had seen my male counterparts act far more arrogantly without write-ups. I had gotten through eight years without a single write-up. But this older nurse would be just the first of many that would feel threatened by another woman. Especially a confident woman.

And so, the big day arrived: graduation, and my proud mother was there. She was talking to my chairman and saying, "Thank you for being so good to her. The first year was really tough, with her dad passing away…" He was surprised; he had never even been aware of this great loss in my life: "She showed up and did her work." And now these eight years of hard work at Parkland had paid off. I was going into the world as a plastic surgeon.

***

I had graduated from medical school when I was twenty-six. Then I did five years of general surgery and three years of plastic surgery residency. I was now thirty-four years old—and very much single. I had been dating throughout my three-year plastic surgery residency after parting ways with my long-time boyfriend from general surgery. Nothing serious. I was too focused on getting through residency and succeeding, and I was selfish about this. I did not have the bandwidth to develop a serious relationship.

This career path is a long road, but a well-defined one, always with the next goal in sight and knowing what needs to be done to reach that next level. At the end of the road, for the first time in your life, you are on the open job market. You have options, choices. There's no longer a defined script, a checklist. It's liberating—but also scary.

As I considered my next move, the one thing I felt sure of was that it was time to leave Parkland. After eight years of living in Dallas, I needed to go. The main concern was geographic: my mother was in the greater NYC area, and I did not want to live so far away from her. I didn't even try to look for a job in Texas, as much as I had grown to love it. It just wasn't in the cards. I wanted more than anything to participate in molding the next generation of plastic surgeons; that was my primary goal when considering where to work.

As a chief resident, my junior residents had called on me frequently to ask for my assistance or advice and asked me to help with particularly difficult cases they were handling. This was a role I loved. I had been fortunate to receive valuable wisdom and experience from my own mentors, which I very much wanted to share with these residents. I knew I was privileged to have a wealth of institutional knowledge and was committed to passing down as much as I could to the next generation. There's a saying in surgery—actually, it's a saying from Sir Isaac Newton, but nonetheless we used it all the time: "If I have seen further, it is by standing on the shoulders of giants."

I had worked and learned from some amazing giants in surgery. They invented procedures, did the groundbreaking studies that changed the standard of care for patients, some of them had even treated JFK all those years back. Some have since retired or passed away, but the lessons I learned were invaluable, and they stayed with me. They had learned from giants, and I was fortunate to have learned from them. I couldn't let that passing on of knowledge stop with me. I had to teach. Nothing could be more gratifying to me as a plastic surgeon.

I had gone to college and medical school in Boston, a place that held many happy memories. When I got an inquiry from a large tertiary-care hospital in that familiar city, I was happy to explore the possibilities. The chair of Surgery at the hospital was an impressive man; he explained that the hospital had no plastic surgery residency at that time. If I came to work there, maybe I could get the ball rolling on a new program. This would be on top of my regular duties in an academic environment where I would be working closely with students and teaching residents. It all sounded ideal. There was so much opportunity here, including the chance to return to the Northeast.

I excitedly talked about the offer and my plans with my plastic surgery mentor in Dallas. He had seen literally thousands of residents through this job-seeking process; he had a sixth sense about what would best suit them. He did not appear particularly enthusiastic about my plan to go to Boston, but he was wise enough not to say anything. He let me talk my way through my decision and supported me as I took my own path and figured things out on my own. While I had some excellent offers from other institutions, none seemed ideal. So, I had made up my mind; there would have been no dissuading me. This was the right place for me, the ideal fit, I was sure of it. I accepted the new job in Boston.

I graduated in June 2014. I'd had a couple weeks off at a time over the past eight years—and this summer was going to be mine. I took July and August off and enjoyed the longest space of free time I'd ever had. I returned to India with my mother to see family and take a true vacation. We had a wonderful time. Then, it was off to my new job—at "home" again.

Reflection:

Confidence in yourself is probably the most important quality you can have as a person. It provides you with a fulfilling life. It can motivate you to take risks or take those small steps that result in big positive changes. It makes you more resilient to failures or hiccups along the way. Confidence leads to more authenticity and deeper relationships.

I find this so appealing as I can honestly say I didn't have much confidence as a young, shy girl.

Confidence-building is the aspect of my job of which I am most proud. I take pride in helping others to achieve confidence through my medical expertise. I see many prospective patients in my own demographic: thirty-, forty-, and fifty-something women. Many are looking to have breast and body work, due to the effects of normal life changes. They want to look and, ultimately, feel their best. Others seek face and neck tweaks. The patients I see for consults are bothered enough, and motivated enough, to do something about these inevitable and normal body changes that can make them feel insecure.

Science supports the mind–body connection, too. A study by the University of Basel and published in Psychological Science found that plastic surgery patients reported significant improvements in self-confidence and enjoyment of life. The research found that their quality of life improved through an improved body image, leading to a boost in their self-esteem.

But not all patients are candidates for plastic surgery. The ideal patient has given serious thought to the pros and cons of surgery, they have appropriate expectations. It isn't an emotional reaction to a breakup, divorce, or personal crisis. And the decision is purely for themselves, with no thought of pleasing anybody else.

I appreciate a patient who has planned for both the expense and time off that surgery requires. All surgeries require some downtime and it's important to set time aside to focus on yourself so that you have the best outcome and can heal well. The time and space to heal is crucial.

Chapter Nine

Operating in the Real Working World

I walked through the doors of a major metropolitan hospital in Boston on my first day of my new job raring to go. I dived in with the highest of hopes. The chair of Surgery at my new hospital was everyone's boss, in charge of the entire surgery department including all its divisions: vascular, colorectal, trauma and plastic surgery. He was a brilliant man and mentor. I was one of four new hires in different specialties; two male and another female surgeon also came on board when I did.

My mandate was plastic surgery. I was to build a reconstructive practice as my interests were in breast reconstruction; reclaim facial cosmetic surgery, which was essentially all given to ENT facial plastics; and build a program in which general surgery residents and plastic surgery fellows from another city hospital rotated with us. This could eventually become the foundation on which to build our own residency program. The chair who had recruited me supported me fully and was helpful and responsive.

Reflection:

Having the support of male colleagues and mentors was not new to me.

I could not have gotten through plastic surgery residency without my male co-residents. Being the only woman in my class and the classes I was sandwiched between could be daunting. My male co-residents were a blessing, they looked after me, and I looked after them. I always felt respected and always had a seat at every table. I can truly say in retrospect that I was not treated differently, I did not have to work twice as hard as the guys, and in most cases was not just given a seat at the table, I was virtually forced to take it.

Gender was simply not a thing during residency. We didn't have time for that. It was only about work, learning, and being the best plastic surgeon. Even back in medical school, my biggest supporter and mentor had been a minimally invasive male surgeon who helped me to forge the path to applying to a general surgery program. This was especially meaningful because I had had a hard time seeing myself as a surgeon since I didn't know anyone that looked like me doing the same. He had encouraged me to follow my dreams and helped me as much as he could in those early years of navigating my career.

My mentors in general surgery and plastic surgery were all men. These guys were my biggest advocates and, to this day, I can turn to them for anything. I never had one moment of feeling "less than." In fact, we used to joke that I was the only girl in the boy's club, and I was proud of that. Other than a few female chief residents when I was a junior in general surgery and one or two attendings, every mentor that I'd ever had in my career to that point had been male. I certainly had no female plastic surgery mentors. I was okay and good with that. This was simply my norm. I didn't realize how helpful certain crucial female relationships would become later in my career.

***

It quickly became clear that "work" was a whole new territory. In residency, as much as you operate, study, learn, and cram, there's a whole lot about actually working as a surgeon you don't encounter. It had all been learning on the job in the hospital, managing patients with acute needs. There was very little exposure to administrative issues like insurance companies or billing or staffing or patient follow-up.

This, I think, is a problem with medical training in general. For us surgeons, there is some exposure to clinics, usually an afternoon or morning a week depending on the rotation. But for all intents and purposes, our job was to learn how to operate. We rarely saw patients after they left the hospital, we didn't have continuity of care, and we certainly did not learn about the business side of medicine. All these concerns and more I was confronted with, immediately. For many of these matters I would go through my immediate boss, my division chief. I wasn't sure the two of us were on the same page, though the chair and I certainly were.

It was a rude shock to find the Boston patient population so challenging compared to Dallas. The issue wasn't the disease process; that remained the same. Here in Boston, patient interactions were rougher. For the first time in my life, I was forcibly reminded just how young and female I really was. I would sit in a patient's room and have forty-five-minute in-depth discussions on the surgery to come. I would detail everything the patient could possibly expect from the upcoming procedure. "This is where your incisions are going to be...this is how you can expect your recovery to proceed..." I never rushed these talks; I always took great pains to explain everything I could.

Several times patients would then say, "OK...so, when is the surgeon coming in to talk to me?" Certainly, I was taken aback, as I had introduced myself as their surgeon and had been sitting there in my white coat with Dr. Ramanadham stitched onto it the entire time.

It was in Boston that I first learned about saying "no" to patients. Sort of. In Dallas, patients were in the hospital or already on the OR schedule because they had urgent medical issues or had already been vetted in clinic by the attending surgeon. When we did say no—for instance, if another doctor had consulted us and surgery was not indicated—patients were usually relieved. That was not the case here.

I had several uncomfortable discussions where I had to tell someone, flat out, that no, I could not perform the surgery he or she desired. The reason might be because the person had a body mass index (BMI) of forty-five, or had uncontrolled cardiac or lung issues that needed to be optimized first. My sound medical reasons for refusing (for now) should have been quite evident, but some of these patients took the refusal badly. They would argue and some would scream and quite literally get in my face.

On multiple occasions I had to step out of the room to grab whomever happened to be in the office and ask them to come in. If that staffer happened to be male—for example, our office manager—then I would get in trouble for bringing a man in the room with a female patient, even though technically the office manager was the next line of contact, as there was typically only one surgeon in clinic at a given time. After a few such encounters I felt I couldn't win this battle. If an irate patient was about to attack me, I needed someone in the room with me. Male or female. Period. End of story.

It was a bumpy beginning to real life on the job, as was returning to Boston to live. I now had culture shock in reverse. It only took a few days for me to realize, "Gosh, everyone is so short and rude here." By this point I automatically smiled at everyone I passed on the street if there was eye contact. On my ten-minute walk from the hospital to the gym my first week on the job I smiled at a man coming toward me as we passed each other. He looked surprised and glanced behind him to see if there was someone else there. I didn't even realize he was a guy until he gave me this weird smirk, thinking I was flirting with him. Oh boy. That was not my intention. I kept moving quickly, and from that point on kept my public smiles to a minimum.

People in Texas would stand at an entrance or exit and wait for you to get to the door to hold it for as long as it took. I was now back in Boston, where doors were regularly slammed in my face as hurried people blew past me. And the city was so crowded and congested; I had become used to the wide-open spaces of Texas. Ironically enough, I really had to wonder: "Why exactly did I ever want to come back here? This is terrible; I should go back to Dallas!"

Work was not without its bright spots. The best thing about my new job, in my academic setting, was that it reaffirmed how much I did love teaching. I was so fulfilled working with the medical students and residents; I loved that part of my duties. But there was so much red tape in this new role. I had not realized how little real autonomy I would have. It became clear quickly that this was just a job—a position where I was not being challenged like I would have liked to be. I was not a trailblazer as much as a cog in an enormous wheel.

It was time for other life changes as well. Being a planner, I had already decided that once residency was over, I'd find my partner in life. How hard could it be? I had dated pretty extensively throughout residency and had ended all those relationships because each was just not the right one. It was a running joke that I left a trail of broken hearts in Dallas. But now, here I was in Boston, ready to settle down. Finally.

I had primarily dated other surgeons. There were pros and cons to this. Marrying a fellow surgeon would mean that medicine and patients would always be a topic of conversation. We would both have grueling schedules, but we would understand that patients were always a priority. I was okay with that. The guys I dated that were not in medicine had less demanding careers, and I just didn't quite click with them professionally. While they were always supportive and ready to listen after a long day at work, I often felt like I had to explain everything too much. It was exhausting to speak to patients all day in layman terms and then come home and speak to my significant other the same way; I couldn't keep from getting annoyed that he didn't just "get it."

The other layer was the traditional gender roles of my Indian upbringing that were always present just under the surface. I couldn't imagine myself being the primary breadwinner in the family. My parents both worked hard and had fulfilling careers. I had always imagined my life with a partner unfolding in the same way. But everyone must find her own way.

I met my possible dates the way every youngish single person did—online. The sifting-out process took up much of my limited spare time. Here in Boston, I didn't have a network of friends as I had had in school or residency; random people all in the same setting that organically became friends. I joined a church singles Bible study; I joined a running group. I met tons of new people and made some great friends. I also met many guys. But didn't meet "my guy" just yet.

***

Every surgeon has his or her own style. When I operate, I am completely focused. I am not there to dilly-dally and make small talk. Some surgeons like to chat, have conversations, some of them may take longer operating because of this small talk. My goal is to get the surgery completed smoothly and the patient off the operating table and safely out of anesthesia. I'm happy to chit-chat for as long as anyone likes in the surgeon's lounge afterward, but not during surgery. In the OR, my priority is my patient. Until the critical portions of the case are done, I'm all business: I have a job to do.

Brand new on the job, my "style" was suddenly causing issues. Some of this stuff was so small and petty, but I found myself having to spend much more time than I would have liked having discussions and meetings about the silliest stuff. Emails I would write to office staff, for example. "They felt you were short and mean in your emails," I was told. I had written an email explaining why clinic patients should not be scheduled while I am in the OR. It seemed fine to me. "Maybe you should just put a smiley face at the end of it?" it was suggested.

Absolutely not. Are you kidding me? *Would you have said this to my male colleagues?* I thought. It was clear to me there would not be such mini drama with my male colleagues. They would not be asked to add smiley faces to their emails because they were too "direct" and therefore possibly offensive. This, to be honest, was a new thought for me. I had never once thought about my experiences based on gender, at least not in my work life. We all had our roles, our responsibilities, male or female, it didn't matter. But suddenly, gender was an issue.

I was finding that some nurses who considered themselves good struggled to keep up with me—my pace, my requests for needles or instruments, for example. Several were not shy about complaining about me to their nurse manager on the floor. This nurse manager, I am happy to say, had my back. "Not sure what they're complaining about," this man said to me during one of our first meetings. "I've seen you operate many times; you keep things moving along. Other surgeons are much more—challenging."

Our plastic surgery physician assistants (PAs) also chimed in, stating that many other male surgeons would get angry and throw instruments or yell and scream. The nurses wouldn't bat an eye, just smile and continue to work. I never raised my voice, yelled or screamed. The PAs seemed surprised by this backlash, they hadn't seen it with the male surgeons. I was equally surprised on the receiving end; I had never encountered these reactions prior to my time in Boston. But other than getting extremely annoyed, I never let it get under my skin. In my opinion, their behavior was a reflection of their own insecurities and biases. I was confident in who I was as a person and surgeon. I handled myself professionally and did not let any of this make me think lesser of myself.

Another day and another meeting with the nurse manager. The latest was, as the manager related the complaint to me, "You were in such a rush and so careless that she stuck herself with a needle." Well, this was a surprise to me because I never even touched that suture. The student scrub tech was practicing how to load a needle onto a needle driver on the back table and stuck herself, on her own. Completely unrelated to me. Yet the scrub tech, who had already had issues with me, thought it would be a great opportunity to file a complaint. Which of course was thrown out due to the absurdity of the whole incident.

Eight years in Dallas without the slightest issue, until that one small incident at the very end. Now such matters were happening on a fairly regular basis. I could not wrap my head around this development, especially as many of the nurses loved working with me and told me so. These were the older, experienced, confident and very good nurses. Male and female. But some did not, and they were quite vocal. I began to feel like I was going crazy.

But I carried on. One day we were doing a tummy tuck. Once a surgeon makes an incision, we use a tool called the electrocautery—an instrument that uses heat from electrical energy to coagulate and cut tissue, essentially, to dissect tissue without causing excessive bleeding. The hospital had recently implemented a new electrocautery that had a suction component built in, so that no one in the OR would have to breathe in any smoke. Unfortunately, this new instrument wasn't working well, so there was a lot of smoke in the room, and some seeped into the hallway.

I was hardly paying attention. I was used to operating without smoke evacuation; I was completely focused on the patient. We were in the middle of an operation. Suddenly, an older nurse burst into my OR and started screaming: "What are you doing in here?! There's smoke everywhere!" I was beyond shocked at her loud, hectoring tone.

"Excuse me? You're coming into my operating room and yelling in the middle of surgery, about, something that is faulty with your instruments?" Obviously, I had not purchased them, or asked to use them. I was operating with the instruments I had at hand. "If there's a problem, you can speak to me after the case or address the issue yourself. But do not come into my room and start yelling while I have a patient I am *actively operating on*!"

We got through the surgery. I was livid. This was a different nurse manager than I had previously worked with. A woman who'd had a problem with me from the beginning. The pattern was becoming hard to ignore. I remembered those words my program director said to me right before I graduated. It all began to make sense: I was a threat, women were intimidated by me, I was the new person who came in with authority as the attending plastic surgeon. It wouldn't have mattered what I said or did, there was going to be a problem.

I'd had just about enough.

***

There was a sea change happening in the work world. The #MeToo movement had started, and new revelations were all over the news, all the time. A friend I had done my general surgery residency with, who now worked as a trauma surgeon in Dallas, and I were talking one night about all that was going on. Of course, we were most interested in the stories that were emerging in surgery.

We'd both heard of our female peers undergoing some terrible experiences of sexual harassment. I knew these complaints were real, as was their suffering, but these women had not been in our own training programs. But as another one of the female minority in a highly male-dominated field, I could not say that I felt the same. I experienced no bullying, no harassment, not even any innuendoes. Any gender issues were much more subtle in my new job. In fact, it was the opposite of #MeToo—as a working surgeon, every time any sort of personnel or administrative dispute came up, it concerned women. Every time.

"Did anything like this happen to us and we just blocked it all out all?" I wondered aloud to my friend. I had definitely been the only woman in my class as a plastic surgery resident, and I had nothing but affection and respect for my male colleagues from that time. "I didn't experience any of this. Did you?" I asked. My friend had been right there with me.

"I thought about this too," she said. "But nothing ever happened like this to us." We were both quiet for a moment, thinking back. Then she joked, "They were probably too scared to mess with us!"

I had a similar conversation with one of my male friends who is now a cardiothoracic surgeon down south. He had been my senior resident on many rotations in general surgery, and we had become close over the years. He, too, wondered if I'd had any bad experiences during training; I confidently told him there was literally nothing I could recall. I had been treated no better, worse, or different than my male colleagues. He also could not recall any instances in which he witnessed such behavior.

Were we just blessed? The many mentors who helped me along the way, from med school onward, were predominately male. My closest friends in the surgical field were male. I would have not been the doctor or surgeon I was without the help and prodding of the many male colleagues who pushed me to do better. The truth is that support and camaraderie is out there with men and women. You must find the good eggs and surround yourself with the right people, male or female. This ongoing national discussion was all an interesting and timely backdrop to my new working world.

Reflection:

Sadly, female medical professionals are not spared the ramifications and career trauma associated with sexual harassment. While I was one of the luckier ones to have only supportive male role models to lean on, I know I am an exception to the rule. New studies show more than half of female physicians will experiences some form of sexual harassment during their career. It's simply inevitable, as the behavior is linked to a hierarchical culture which is prevalent in medicine.

Dr. Nell Maloney Patel, a colorectal surgeon and president of the medical staff executive committee at Robert Wood Johnson University Hospital at Rutgers is an inspirational figure to me and so many of my female counterparts. She gives us all a glimmer of hope as she believes there are big changes on the horizon.

Like myself, she feels lucky to have had good mentors in medical school, where she studied minimally invasive and robotic surgery. She was the first female surgeon to become a professor at her institute, which is not surprising given only 21 percent of women make it to associate professor, and then the numbers continue to drop off as leadership hierarchy increases.

While she herself did not experience sexual harassment, bullying or disrespect, like myself, we are an exception to the rule. She attests that most female surgeons experience some form of bias due to their gender. Discrepancies can come in all shapes and forms. Whether it is a salary inequity, managing the implicit biases of patients and those around us, or using equipment not made for our sized hands, almost everyone has a story that matches this narrative. But, Dr. Patel believes the environment is changing as more women enter surgery.

Regarding interactions with patients, she says patients often benefit from having a female surgeon, including a reduced risk of postoperative complications, according to the data. Research has also found that, in general, patients of female surgeons have lower rates of mortality, readmission and other adverse complications. The reason: It is believed that communication style has an impact on these outcomes.

***

There was one last hurdle for me to clear, though I was already working full-time as a plastic surgeon: board certification. Plastic surgery boards are taken in two parts. Written boards first, that test your clinical knowledge. Once you pass that come the oral boards, a series of in-person examinations over a two-day period ascertaining that you are a skilled and safe surgeon. This includes two sessions of unknown cases—basically, you are in a hotel room with two board examiners who ask you surgical and patient-care questions about random cases.

They may show you a picture of a complex hand injury and you're expected to explain how you would care for this patient. They might throw complications or other curveballs at you to see how you would manage them. Another session includes a careful review of your collected cases, which you have gathered, prepared, and submitted to the board in advance. You cannot even sit for the orals until you have at least fifty of your own surgeries to be submitted to the board for evaluation.

I passed the written boards but would not take my oral boards until a full year had passed working at my first job. No matter how well or poorly things might have been going in my new position, I was committed to taking and passing those oral boards. To leave your position early can make the oral boards more challenging than they already are. It would require having to explain to the board why I left but, even more difficult, I would have lost the ability to follow up on my patients. The follow-up or postoperative-care documentation is needed for all submitted cases in addition to photographs. Leaving this job would in all likelihood result in me delaying boards for at least another year. This was not a good plan; I would be sticking out my new job for at least a year, no matter what!

***

By the time my boards were over I was two years into my job and growing unhappier by the month. At this point I began actively looking for other positions. I had stayed in touch with my former mentors in Dallas, all of whom wanted me to return as a faculty member at Parkland. Once I officially passed my boards, they reached out to me formally. "Come back and interview." So, over a long November weekend I flew back for a series of interviews. This process was incredibly fun. I was able to see all my colleagues, friends, and mentors who made me the doctor and plastic surgeon I now was; every meeting was with someone I had worked alongside for years. It was homecoming, pretty much, and all signs pointed to them welcoming me back with open arms.

A true mentor to me, a man I considered almost a grandfather figure in terms of his advice and guidance over the years, pulled me aside after all the interviews were concluded. I trusted this man implicitly; he was one of the giants in surgery that I that I respected enormously. During my last interview of the day, we heard a knock. Ten minutes in, he entered the room and told my interviewer, “She’s coming with me.” There was a faculty dinner that night, as was tradition for any surgical attending applicant. We were heading to the restaurant early to grab a drink before everyone else showed up.

We sat at the bar; I was excited to catch up with him. And he didn’t waste any time. “Did you reach out to our Chairman about a job?” he asked.

“No, I’ve been texting with all of my old attendings from UT Southwestern since I graduated. Every 6 a.m. faculty meeting included getting text messages from random attendings gauging my interest.” Of course I was interested, I was not happy at my current job. All the things I’d hoped for at my position in Boston simply didn’t exist as they did at Parkland.

The available job in Dallas was a combination role in which 70 percent to 80 percent of my time would be spent at Parkland Hospital, primarily teaching reconstructive surgery, with the remainder of my time at UT Southwestern, where I could build my own cosmetic practice. “What does the Parkland job mean to you?” he probed me as soon as we got our drinks. As I tried to put it into words, a light bulb came on. He noticed. “Your Botox is overdue,” he said jokingly. My thoughts were evidently written all over my face.

To do the Parkland job well, I would have to be hands-off in all the right ways. Parkland had one of the few remaining residency programs at the time where the faculty were present, but not nearly as hands-on as other programs across the country. Occasionally they would scrub in for surgery, but the idea was very much about promoting the resident's work. Parkland was the place we truly learned how to become surgeons. The more autonomy we were allowed, the better and stronger we became. This role required 100 percent commitment. The residents and patients deserved this. There was no way to be half in and half out as I tried to build a side cosmetic practice. The numbers didn't quite work out.

In addition to all that, I knew from my eight years there how late Parkland OR days could go. I could be there all day and well into the evening, every evening. Far later than I would be if I were operating and doing the cases on my own. To top it off, this position would require no less than a ten-year commitment. I would be moving my life back to Dallas for the foreseeable future. This, I was not opposed to: I missed Dallas.

My mentor and I talked through every scenario; more drinks were on their way. He made things as clear as could be about how my day-to-day would play out. Blue ill-fitting scrubs, hair in a bun, no true connection with patients. I liked dressing up and putting myself together. More important, I didn't want to give up performing cosmetic surgery. I liked the finesse and attention to detail of those surgeries. I loved making patients feel more confident and self-assured.

He knew this. He'd known all this years ago when I sat in his office every Friday afternoon as a chief resident. He smirked, the "finally you get it" smile. I wished he had just told me this years ago—he would have saved me years of not being happy or fulfilled at my job. But like any good teacher, he needed me to come to that realization myself. Which I did, that night.

The other faculty slowly started to trickle in. "If you say anything, I'll deny every word," he whispered to me with a smile, as he toasted me one last time and we joined the already seated table of my mentors and friends.

***

I flew home very torn. I wasn't happy where I was, but I wasn't actively looking at other positions besides the one in Dallas at this point so there was no relief in sight. I didn't want to jump from one ship to another one without being 100 percent sure. UT Southwestern bridges were those I couldn't risk burning. After some agonizing I decided *not* to take the position at Parkland in Dallas. As is the case with most things, there were little signs in Boston that all the work I had been doing until then was finally coming to fruition. The laser I had so painstakingly tried to get purchased finally got approval. The Lahey Clinic in Burlington, MA had its own plastic surgery residency and those plastic surgery residents were also finally approved to start rotating at my institution in Boston. I just had to ride it out.

Another year came and went. Then our chairman in Boston, the man who played a big factor in my accepting my current job in Boston, was heavily recruited and lured away to a new position at another big Boston hospital. When he left, there was interim chairman for a year or so before the new female chairwoman eventually arrived, but by this time, three years into practice, I was completely disillusioned. I felt alone without any support. There was nobody who understood the issues I was having. I didn't have any mentors in this institution which is a tremendous detriment to any young academic surgeon. It was now time to do something else.

Reflection:

"Gaming everything out" will likely sound very familiar for anyone practicing medicine. That is because in the medical field there is a very specific path to success, with a list of boxes to be checked off in order. Get into a good college so you can get into a good medical school—but only if you do well in your classes and your MCATs. Next, get into a good residency program—but only if you do well in medical school and your USMLE exams. Once you're in residency, take the best care of your patients and learn as much as you can because, inevitably, you'll be out on your own with people's lives in your hands and may still need to get into a good and reputable fellowship program.

Then you are done and you have options. Options of where to work, whom to work for, or to go out on your own. It's the first time we had to make big decisions based on our specialty. It was daunting, but I received some great advice from my program director and vice-chairman in Dallas: "You have to make the best decision for yourself right now. This is the only information you have. If you need to pivot and change course later, that's okay." I carried those life-changing words with me during those years I was unfilled and unhappy in Boston.

While doctors are constantly planning and gaming things out, I believe this is a trait shared by anyone successful in their field. Always thinking about the next step, the next goal, the bigger and better pillar and setting yourself up for that now. You must be open to change and never put yourself in a situation where doors may be closed.

Chapter Ten

My Name on the Door: Building My Own Brand

Professionally, I simply wasn't fulfilled in Boston. In fact, I thought I may have gotten it all completely wrong. Maybe I'd been so obsessed with succeeding on a certain path (pre-med, med school, surgery residency, plastic surgery) that I'd never had a clear view of where I was headed. Maybe I didn't even like plastic surgery, after all.

But I soon realized that I very much enjoyed attending plastic surgery medical conferences where I got to learn new techniques and procedures. I loved hearing the buzz about what was new in our world and connecting with my colleagues in the field. It was just that every time I returned from such a gathering, I'd go back to work and immediately feel utterly deflated. It wasn't the field; mine was clearly a situational issue.

Reflection:

In the late 2010's, burnout on the job was finally becoming a concern, especially in the medical field. The rate of burnout amongst physicians as a whole was approaching 50 percent; with plastic surgery practitioners not far behind at 37 percent. There are multiple reasons for this, in my opinion. As doctors we are trained to always put the patient first, which oftentimes comes at the expense of our own health. We ignore necessities, such as sleep, food, and even using the restroom if there is work to be done and patients to be cared for. This has been ingrained in us since our clinical rotations in medical school. You were considered a weak resident if you needed to excuse yourself or complained about anything. You just forged ahead despite the toll that work took on you. These were traits we all carried with us into the work force. Those tendencies with the added stress of not being prepared for the work force exponentially added to the rate of burnout.

Simply put: residency does not prepare you for the business of medicine. Sure, you're a great clinical doctor, but now you are dealing with reimbursements, insurance companies, Press Ganey scores. These are scores obtained from surveys in which patient satisfaction is assessed, ranging from office wait times to their experience with the office and your care. Oftentimes, physician promotions are tied to these results. You have to negotiate and advocate for yourself. These are skills we were never taught—which sets new doctors up for burnout.

Eventually institutions realized that this was a growing issue and required educational training to reduce physician burnout. This required training backfired as it was yet another pressing demand on a doctors' already limited time. It's so important in every field to realize that unless you are refueled, you cannot give more of yourself to anyone, including your patients. It's not a weakness to spend time with your family, to say no to speaking at a conference, and to take time off. These are mechanisms to fill your cup so that you can be your best for your patients. I would have to address my own serious burnout before even considering where to land next.

It wasn't just me: burnout was becoming a topic that people were beginning to talk about in our profession. The more I learned about the issue, the more I realized I was a classic case. I was completely burned out only two or three years into my career! I needed to leave my current job in Boston. So, I started to look at other academic jobs after deciding against returning to Parkland. As always, I carefully considered every option, including moving to Miami to join the practice of one of my mentors, whom I respected greatly.

I realized that in any of these options I would still be working for somebody else, and that's what my entire future really came down to: I not only wanted to be a plastic surgeon, I wanted to call the shots. I wanted to build a practice I could run, and build a brand I could be proud of. I had a vision. I needed autonomy. But when I floated this idea, I got a lot of pushback. Again, I was hearing the word "no." I talked it over with my mother who said, "We did this back in the eighties but now medicine is an entirely different field. Do you really want to do this? *Can* you actually do this?"

My dad had been the doer, the man who executed the plans. Had he been around, he would certainly have gotten my practice up and running with me. That would have been ideal. But he was gone. "Just be sure you know what you are getting yourself into," she warned me.

"Thanks for the vote of confidence, Mom," I said with a sigh.

My close guy friends, also surgeons, weighed in. "Are you sure? You're going to want to have kids soon, it'll be hard to take time off. You'll have to be on call every day and weekends for your patients." This was not untrue.

I joined the WPS Committee—Women in Plastic Surgery—by default. A mentor suggested it as I was trying to get more involved in our national society. I didn't think I needed to be a part of an all-female group. I had more mentors than I could count on all fingers and toes. All of them were men. They had been with me every step of the way. But I was saying "yes" to everything at this stage of my career. Little did I know that joining this group of amazing women would absolutely save me and change the entire course of my professional life.

The WPS Committee held a weekend-long annual meeting every February in various locations throughout the country. I had been to several meetings in the past. It was a small conference at the time, with many of the same women attending every year; I had started to get to know some of them.

Reflection:

As a woman, it's important to have some female mentors. Looking back, one of the hardest decisions during my schooling was choosing surgery. I didn't have any female surgeons to look up to. They all were "not nice" and did not have good reputations. I couldn't see a life as a surgeon when I was twenty-five. I was fortunate, though. I was surrounded by stellar male colleagues and mentors. But I didn't know what I was missing when it came to female mentors. Someone who had similar challenges in the work force, shared issues with finding life partners, fertility, or starting families. Female mentors, colleagues, and friends are invaluable. They can be your biggest supporters, your tribe, your cheerleaders. I'm grateful for mine. Conversations with them changed the trajectory of my career. The light bulb went on.

One particular year I found myself at the annual conference in snowy, beautiful Banff in Alberta. I would overhear side conversations where these women talked about issues they had at their own jobs, with their staff and nurses. It was harassment and discrimination but not in the traditional way. These women were experiencing what I was coming to find was also a norm in medicine. Women hating on women. "Wait, I'm not the only one?" I thought. I truly didn't realize other people—other *female surgeons*—were experiencing what I was: completely unexpected treatment in the workplace at the hands of other women. I was being treated differently – and much more poorly – than my male colleagues.

All I had done so far was vent to my guy friends who were supportive and great listeners. They would get mad on my behalf, but they could only relate so far as they didn't personally experience this particular issue. We would end our conversations concluding that it was situational, a problem at my particular institution. It wasn't. This was a much bigger issue that many women were facing.

During lunch one day I was sitting with two women I had looked up to since I was a resident. While I had never met them formally prior to joining WPS, I had seen them in various meetings as a resident and truly respected them. These two surgeons mentioned that they used to work at this or that hospital or university, which I was shocked to hear, as I had only known them to have thriving solo practices. I had never imagined they dealt with the same things I had. They seemed happy and fulfilled.

I finally got up the courage to tell them about what I had been facing. The backlash, the undermining, the smiley faces in emails. It was endless. I felt hopeless. There was no support and certainly no one on my side. They had all been there. These two women had literally been in my shoes in the past and lived through very similar experiences with the nurses, the patients, and their superiors. *What a relief to realize I was not alone.*

"I just left. I opened my own practice. I can do whatever I want whenever I want, I have all the flexibility in the world," one of them said. "I've never been happier. If this is what you want to do, then you need to do it. You will never look back! We're here to help you."

These two female plastic surgeons, both about ten years older than me, planted the seed and encouraged me greatly. My friend, another female plastic surgeon, was experiencing many of the same issues I was at another university program. We were both feeling the same way: creatively and professionally stifled. We took a big leap and made the transition together. She wound up joining a group practice in New York, and I decided to go out on my own. It would come together for both of us. We had no other choice.

***

I had been dating the same man for three years at this point. We eventually got engaged, but at the time I could not make my decision on where to open my own practice based on him. I had no desire to open a practice in Boston; if I was going to open my own practice, I would move to Dallas, where I had a network and understood the plastic surgery environment, or to New Jersey, where my mother lived along with one of my closest longtime friends. My boyfriend and I explored both options with a trip to Dallas and another to New Jersey to look at different neighborhoods. Ultimately, New Jersey seemed like the best bet. My mom would always be available if I was in a bind, and she had office space I could use as I got started. New Jersey was also just a stone's throw away from New York and Boston.

Luckily, my boyfriend was quite supportive of my plan. It was his idea to look into New Jersey to begin with, a place that wasn't even on my radar. I never in a million years thought I would end up back in New Jersey. But it made sense for him and for me and so I pulled the trigger and resigned from my position.

My last day at my job in Boston was a big relief. As I exited the building for the last time my only thought was, "I will never have to walk through these doors again!" It was the happiest, most liberating feeling. It had been a true learning experience, and I would never regret my time there. I ultimately had to go through this experience to end up where I am today, but after four and half years it was time for something new. I was going to open my own practice. I was going to be a business owner. I was going to do things on my own terms.

***

As I have probably made clear by now, surgeons are nothing if not planners. We need to feel confident that we know everything there is to know about our work, inside and out. We are experts. We don't have a choice. We are operating on human beings. But here I was trying to open a business. I had to write a business plan. How do you do that? That phrase "paralysis by analysis" applied to me. I was trying to learn everything before I executed. Not possible.

My boyfriend tried to coach me. He was not in medicine. "Use your resources, the people who are the experts, and just do it. It may not be perfect, but perfection doesn't exist." And so I did. I wrote a business plan. Then came the rest. The waiting. There was lots of waiting and many delays. It took months for a permit to start construction, for example, and there was absolutely nothing I could do to speed that and many other processes along.

I had assumed I could easily (and quickly) get privileges at some nearby New Jersey–area hospitals. That process turned into a weeks- and months-long application ordeal. What I thought I could accomplish in six months stretched into more than a year. For a surgeon to not be in control and unable to do anything to impact the outcome is very stressful, and I lived that for a year. It was a very long year!

Then there was the matter of finding patients. In Boston, I had been one of three plastic surgeons at my hospital, and all patients were internally referred. My two colleagues and I only had to operate on them. Now, I had to find a patient base, which is always the bottom line for anyone opening a business. Finding their own patients is not a situation many doctors are accustomed to. I also had to come up with a marketing and advertising strategy and hire staff; all new brand-new challenges I was facing without my father's business expertise.

The answer for me was networking and more networking. I began by establishing a presence on social media. I built on this by going around to all the local hospitals in person and offering to give talks. It was a long and painstaking year of slow building. The last day at my job in Boston had been in October 2018, and I had confidently predicted that by April or May 2019, I'd be ready to go. That didn't happen.

Still, the doors to my very own practice with my logo SR (my initials) on the door opened in November 2019 in East Brunswick to serve the central Jersey area. I threw a grand opening party in January with the mayor of the town, right after New Year's, and we got off to a good and steady start. Then along came COVID-19. I had quit my job, moved to New Jersey, planned for more than a year, and finally managed to open an office with the help of my only employee. Overnight, we were shut completely down from March 2020 through the end of June due to the pandemic. That was more than a little scary for a fledgling business. I couldn't say my timing was great.

I was fortunate that, through a PPP loan, I could pay that one salary; otherwise, I would have had to immediately lay off my sole employee. So, to sum up: I had expenses without revenue. No patients equaled no business. We used that time to retrench, watching webinars on best business practices. We learned as much as we could. I needed to stay relevant and find a way to help the community as well. We offered concierge services to patients who had fallen, for example, and sustained cuts, so that they did not have to go to the ER to have them sutured. We sold skin care products and shipped directly to our patients' homes while educating them on social media about the importance of a good skin care routine.

This was also the time I started a podcast with my friend Ashley to provide our patients and viewers with authentic plastic surgery information while promoting the work of female plastic surgeons. We started as an Instagram live and quickly transitioned to YouTube. We were even featured on *The Doctors* talk show once quarantine ended.

But here was the unexpected silver lining: after three months stuck at home, everybody in America had been watching themselves on Zoom calls and in many cases not liking what they saw on their computer screens. COVID-19 gave everybody plenty of time at home to stare straight in the mirror. Because they couldn't travel or go out to eat or shop, many people had some disposable money saved. When my office was allowed to reopen, elective surgery was where they wanted to spend it.

As a doctor, in general, this was a bad time for my profession. Several surgeons I knew who were just a couple of years away from retirement wound up closing their practices for good during the pandemic. They ran large well-established businesses with a lot of overhead, and being unable to perform surgeries put them in an untenable bind. I was extremely busy the summer after quarantine ended with a lot of business, I was not sure would have come my way had my brand-new launch not been interrupted by COVID. In my specialty, there was newfound demand for cosmetic surgery. Everyone wanted to feel confident and get out there again This was the silver lining.

***

Reflection:

It was way back in college that I began to develop my time management skills. My course load between pre-med, economics, and art history did not overlap. I had to juggle my studies and exams while having some semblance of a social life. These skills set me up for success in medical school, where the sheer volume of information we had to learn in a short period of time was unimaginable. With each new phase of life on the path to becoming a plastic surgeon came more responsibility, more studies, and more demands on my time.

Today I'm the founder and owner of a plastic surgery practice and manage two thriving locations. It's not that I am so special or that different from others, but there is certainly something to be said for time management, organization, and efficiency. I have always found that the more time I have, the less efficient I am. I only procrastinate when I have the time to do so! The busier I am, the more I accomplish. Time management is another of those skills (like planning) I would bet nearly every successful person has mastered, no matter what her field. Time is such a limited resource, which makes it invaluable. Time goes by much too fast, and it's something we can never get back. Therefore, time should be used wisely.

If you have a goal in mind—mine was to become a top-notch plastic surgeon—then set mini-goals for yourself first. My original mini-goal was to become board certified in general surgery. The next was making it through that first, most difficult year of my plastic surgery residency. Breaking up this long, long path with mini-goals made each step more palatable and attainable. Just as I did when I ran into all kinds of delays and frustrations along the path to setting up my own practice, I got through one hurdle at a time. Similar to what James Clear advocates in his bestselling book Atomic Habits: *set small habits, these small habits eventually turn into something big. This involves discipline, managing every minute of your day well, and always keeping that distant big goal in mind.*

My long-term boyfriend and I became engaged shortly after my move to New Jersey, however, our relationship was one of the relationships that did not survive COVID, and when I eventually decided to try the dating world again, it was online. Once again, I was open to dating men with professions outside of medicine. I met Andrew, a finance guy, the year after COVID. He was from Pennsylvania originally, from a family who had been in the area for many, many generations and grew up in Connecticut. He now worked on Wall Street in institutional equity sales.

On our first date at a restaurant, he offered, "Do you want to just order a few dishes and share?" "Sounds good, order whatever, I don't really care," I told him. He was a little surprised. "You don't care what you *eat?*" I thought that was an odd question, but no, I'm not a picky eater. I don't think it's possible for a surgeon to be one. We were lucky if we even had time to eat while on call. We survived on hospital graham crackers and saltines, peanut butter, and ginger ale during residency. There was no way we could possibly be picky when it came to food. "Not at all," I replied.

As a surgeon, and now as the boss of a growing small business, I was always in charge. Making every decision about my patients' care and the day-to-day workings in the office. In the OR, as the head surgeon, you are the leader of the team in that room. Everyone looks to you for any issue, concern, or decision. At home, I wanted the opposite. If it wasn't important (the food I ordered off the menu, for example) I didn't want anything to do it with it. Andrew came through and, crazily, it was one of the traits that most appealed to me as we started to see each other frequently. He took charge of any and all arrangements. I didn't have to make any decisions or put any time into thinking about our dates. I just had to show up dressed appropriately at the correct time. It was spectacular!

Andrew was constantly working too; he had to be available for his clients at all hours. He would listen as I vented a bit about work and comment, but I didn't feel the need to overexplain everything. He was in a completely different but equally taxing and time-consuming career; he got it. It was a good match; we just clicked.

The way we had grown up was culturally different; in two different worlds, really, as he had the classic sports-playing, suburban Connecticut "all-American" childhood. But his father, a pediatric nephrologist and chief of Pediatrics at the local hospital, had also been enormously influential in his life. Like me, he had lost his dad at much too early an age. These were key bonding factors for both of us as we became more serious. Andrew had revered his father and was very close to his mother and two siblings, just as I was close to my own family. In many ways, we were the perfect match.

***

Indian weddings are very Hindu-focused, and both my husband and I had been raised as Christians. Our wedding ceremony was Christian, on the beach with our closest friends and family in attendance, though we threw in some Indian traditions. In our *Haldi* ceremony the day before our wedding, we did a traditional Indian purification, where the family applies turmeric on the couple to symbolize cleansing, protection, and blessings for a prosperous marriage while feeding us fruits and sweets. The idea is that both bride and groom are starting the marriage with a clean slate with their families behind them supporting them. It was the perfect blend of our Christian faith and my Indian culture.

My new husband and I settled in Montclair, New Jersey. It had been important to me that my spouse be open to having kids. I was realistic about our chances given my age—late thirties—so Andrew and I met with a fertility doctor recommended by my OB/GYN before we married knowing that this could be a long journey. It was. I remained optimistic—reproductive medicine and fertility treatments had advanced significantly in recent years since the time I had looked into freezing my eggs—something I'd ultimately decided against. If it was God's plan for me to have kids, it would happen.

Now I was married, my practice was established, and our new home all set up and ready to welcome a baby. Yet, things didn't go as I had planned. We tried to conceive for months; for years, in fact. IUI, IVF, failed embryo transfers—you name the procedure, we tried it. The shots, the pills, the appointments, rescheduling my patients because timing is so critical. I was happy to do this even though the heartache was nearly unbearable many times when we experienced yet another disappointment. It didn't make it any easier that I was in medicine and truly understood our chances. At one point, I even miscarried. We were devastated—but the story of having kids is far from over.

Reflection:

When I met with a fertility specialist (long before I met my husband) and had the initial testing, it all seemed to be a numbers game, a game of chance. There was no guarantee that after all the expenses and invasive egg harvests that these eggs would survive the thaw, fertilization, implantation, or become a baby. I was not the ideal age either, as the best time to freeze eggs is in your twenties, and I was already thirty-five. This was simply not the right option or time for me. Looking back, I can't say I regret that decision; I did the best I could based on the information I had.

As I have said throughout this book, I am a firm believer that God has a plan for each of us in life. Mine has taken some twists and turns I never expected; this is just one more. If a child is meant to be; it will be. I have every confidence it will turn out as it should.

Fertility in surgery is a true issue. When I was a resident, these issues were not discussed. We were in medical school and residency during the most fertile years of our lives, our twenties. We had grueling schedules, no sleep, unhealthy diets, radiation exposure (although limited if we were careful and wore lead vests during X-rays, and continual stress. It is a known fact that women in medicine altogether have higher infertility rates across the board.

I went through my entire twenties and early thirties believing that when I was ready to have children, I would.

Just like everything else in my life, I had planned and prepared for this moment. If I planned and prepared, it would happen as expected. Of course, this is not always the case. And while fertility was not discussed during my years in training, things are changing. Fertility treatments have significantly advanced, including the ability to freeze eggs for future use. There is far more awareness; it's now part of the conversation. This is invaluable, and I hope that any young woman who reads this book at least considers and looks into her fertility options earlier rather than later.

***

Meanwhile work was all-consuming. My commute to East Brunswick every day quickly became too much. I was spending three solid hours a day in the car navigating the Garden State Parkway, where an accident or two is a given every single day. I never made it home before 7 p.m., exhausted and cranky from the long commute.

My husband didn't understand why I was driving myself into the ground driving to central New Jersey every day when we lived in an affluent town in North Jersey that was growing increasingly popular, with a consistent influx of New Yorkers moving in. "Just open another office here."

Easier said than done. I was finally established in East Brunswick; I had a good solid practice and needed to keep it going. And so, for a solid year, I made the drive until I had had enough. I opened a second location in Montclair, which I kept open once a week.

"The more time you spend in that East Brunswick office, the more business will come to you, and you're going to get stuck. Your new place here in Montclair won't ever get busy if you're never here. Rip the band-aid off. Patients will follow," my husband advised.

What he said made sense, and I now run two offices in New Jersey. On any given day, the clinic schedule always falls around the OR schedule, which varies per week. If I'm operating, I'm up at 5 a.m., have some coffee, and drive to the hospital and scrub in for 7 a.m. surgery. Depending on how long it takes or how many surgeries I have, I might see patients in the afternoon for consults or follow-ups. If it's a clinic day, depending on which location I'm in, the day starts a bit later. I get up, work out first (I am a committed morning workout person), and head out to see patients.

I enjoy the variety in my days: seeing new prospective patients, doing a couple of small procedures—some Botox, fillers—then some follow ups. It breaks up the days, and I enjoy them all, from mommy makeovers to menopause makeovers and the increasing number of male patients, too! All of them need a boost, and that's what I'm here to offer.

***

The other day, well into my early 40's, I hit the gym hard early in the morning. The lighting in gyms is always particularly terrible and in that harsh glare it was very apparent to me: I would soon need an upper-lip lift and a facelift. It wouldn't be long. I immediately texted my friend in Dallas who now specializes in facial aesthetics. I had known him a long time. He was my co-resident back in the day and someone I would absolutely trust with my own face. "The time for my facelift is getting nearer, be ready," I joked. When I feel it's time, I won't hesitate.

And again, this is something that gives my patients a sense of comfort: I know exactly what's happening to their faces and bodies as they age. I often have the same concerns about myself that they do about themselves. I can relate.

I walked into my office to prepare to see patients for the day and looked at a gift on a shelf in my personal office; something I see every day. This was one of the most meaningful gifts I have ever received—from my brother upon my graduation from my general surgery residency. It is an empty bottle of medication—one my dad used to manufacture in his facility—encased in a plastic block with the caption "Be like Dad."

My dad had wanted so badly to be a surgeon. It simply wasn't in the cards, and, instead, he made medications that helped and healed hundreds and thousands of people. His reach was far. He affected so many lives for the better; it isn't always just the one-on-one interaction of a doctor with his patient that matters. Every time I see this pill bottle, I consider the next step in my path. It all comes back to this: how can I make a bigger difference?

While I can't operate on more than one person at a time, and my relationships with my patients are very personal, I often think about how I can make a bigger difference. I think, for me, that the next step includes educating and advocating for patients on a bigger platform, where the reach is so influential. The primary reason why I took my first job, an academic position in Boston, was so I could teach the next generation of plastic surgeons. While I still teach residents on a less formal and smaller scale, teaching and educating the public has become so important to me. Unfortunately, in the era when everyone is an expert on social media and Dr. Google is more trusted than the actual medical doctor, there is so much misinformation circulating. Reaching the public on a grander scale on television has been a privilege that I hope to continue in the future. In fact, I would love to be a medical correspondent for a national television show.

Meanwhile, I love and keep busy with my work in the beauty and makeup industry. This industry is a multibillion-dollar global industry. Many women and men turn to makeup and skin care to feel their best. A similarity between this and my role as a plastic surgeon. I've had the honor and privilege to serve as a consultant and an advisory board member for IT Cosmetics, a Loreal company. I am delighted to be part of the product development process. I think it's important for people to use the right products with the right ingredients for their skin health. In the future, it is another dream of mine to have a bigger role with a worldwide makeup brand—or even better to continue with and expand my role at IT Cosmetics.

All these thoughts and more run through my head every morning as I see this precious gift. Then I speak to my scheduler about who's coming in first. Will it be a young woman who is just starting preventative Botox and a lifetime of good skin habits and preservation? A woman in her late fifties seeking a facelift? A mom in her thirties who wants a semblance of her pre-baby body back? I'm here and ready. Whom and how will I help today?

Afterword

Across the board in every area of medicine, patients tend to gravitate to doctors who come from their own ethnic background for the reassuring relatability factor. My mom, herself an Indian doctor, only worked with other Indian physicians for her entire life. As I got older and established my own medical career many times, I'd tell my mom that she needed to choose her doctors based on where they trained and not just because they were Indian or were her friends. She would always agree with me on some level. Still, Mom always wound right back with her trusted Indian practitioners for whatever she or Dad needed. The Indians ahead of me—particularly those in my parents' generation—tend to have the same mentality as my mom. They have comfort and trust in someone with the same background. Time and time again, Indian patients have chosen me because I am Indian. They are confident that I know how to treat their darker skin and understand how their skin will heal due to melanin and other genetics. Their skin will act and react the same way my own skin will. For example, I know that certain lasers or chemical peels will work much better on darker complexions than other lasers and peels. My Indian patients feel comfort in this. This advantage is something that I don't take lightly. We see this regularly in other minorities as well. The relatability, the comfort, and similar cultural and ethical norms make it inevitable

The numbers of South Asians living in America are significant, with 5.4 million in 2018, a 40 percent growth since 2010. It is projected that South Asians will be the largest immigrant population in this country by 2065—and they will seek out doctors with whom they feel a connection. Already many Indian-trained doctors make up a large component of international medical graduates in the United States. They fill a gap in medical care created by the capping of available medical school spots and the ever-growing population and aging of the baby boomers.

I am rooting for all the young aspiring female Indian doctors who may pursue plastic surgery as their calling. By improving our diversity numbers, we will help in improving access to every area of health care among minority populations. I am proud to have become a plastic surgeon when it was much more unusual. As time passes, we plastic surgeons should be reflective of and representative of this country's diversity. Those of us that have made it or are making it through, and have tackled our own hurdles, should always extend a hand back to the younger generations. It's more than our duty—it's a privilege.

Acknowledgments

The idea for this book started with a quick side conversation I had at a work event with one of my husband's colleagues. He urged me to write a book. He had seen my previous television appearances and thought this would be a great next step. My initial instinct was what an absurd suggestion that was, so I took those words lightly. Later that evening, I shared this crazy idea with my husband, Andrew, who without hesitation thought it was a great idea. After some brainstorming, I mentioned it to my publicist, Mindie, who I had worked with for several years to market my brand and practice. Her excitement only fueled my desire to share my story. They all deserve a huge thank you. I would not be writing this without their initial encouragement!

A special thank you to Anthony Ziccardi, Caitlin Burdette, and the team at Post Hill Press for taking a chance on a plastic surgeon with a dream of writing a book to inspire young women around the world, not only in my own profession but in any male-dominated field.

Thank you to Julie McCarron who was instrumental in the writing of this book, whose enthusiasm immensely helped to combat my moments of imposter syndrome.

Thank you to my friends, my chosen family. Thank you for making life fun and for keeping me sane. I love you all.

About the Author

Author Photo by
Priyanca Rao

Dr. Smita R. Ramanadham is a board-certified plastic surgeon and founder of SR Plastic Surgery P.C., a boutique aesthetic practice with two locations in Montclair and East Brunswick, New Jersey. She additionally serves on the Advisory Board of IT Cosmetics where she co-develops makeup and skin care for this global brand.

Dr. Ramanadham graduated with her undergraduate degree in economics and art history and her doctorate of medicine degree from Tufts University and Tufts University School of Medicine in Boston, Massachusetts. She then went on to complete her general surgery and plastic and reconstructive surgery training at the prestigious University of Texas Southwestern in Dallas, Texas. Prior to moving back to her home state of New Jersey, Dr. Ramanadham was an Assistant Professor of Surgery at Boston University/ Boston Medical Center, where she cared for the underserved population of Boston and taught aspiring plastic surgeons.

Dr. Ramanadham is a Fellow of the American College of Surgeons, serves as an active member of the American Society of Plastic Surgeons (ASPS), The Aesthetic Society, and serves on multiple national committees. Additionally, Dr. Ramanadham is a former member of the editorial board for *Plastic and Reconstructive Surgery* and Advances in Cosmetic Surgery. She serves as a chair for the ASPS Oral Board Preparation Course. She is well-published in peer-reviewed journals and textbooks and has been regularly featured in the media including *Good Morning America, The Tamron Hall Show*, CBS, FOX5, PIX11, The Doctors, *NY Post, Daily Mail, The Washington Post*, and *Vogue*. You can find her every week on *Lipstick & Lipo: Your Unfiltered Guide to Plastic Surgery*, a podcast and YouTube show that dives deep into plastic surgery, pop news, and navigating a career in medicine as female plastic surgeons.

Her professional passions include supporting other women navigate cultural and gender related issues in the workforce and believes that mentorship is vital for personal success. When asked what her favorite surgery is, the answer is simple, the one that allows her patients to look and feel their best. She considers it a privilege and honor to help her patients feel their most confident.

In her free time, Dr. Ramanadham is an avid runner and has completed five marathons, including four world majors. She is an Orangetheory enthusiast, loves to travel the world with her husband, and is trying to "pick up" golf.

She continues to "work hard, play hard."

www.ingramcontent.com/pod-product-compliance
Lightning Source LLC
LaVergne TN
LVHW050646100826
845148LV00011B/2003

* 9 7 9 8 8 9 5 6 5 2 1 5 2 *